Training Guide
MS-DOS 5 & 6

Clifford Mould

PITMAN
PUBLISHING

PITMAN PUBLISHING
128 Long Acre, London WC2E 9AN
A Division of Longman Group UK Limited

© Longman Group UK Limited 1994

First published in Great Britain 1994

British Library Cataloguing in Publication Data
A CIP catalogue record for this book is available
on request from the British Library.

ISBN 0-273-60059-1

Printed in England by Clays Ltd, St Ives plc

Contents

Section E   Configuring MS-DOS   89

Introduction

The purpose of this Training Guide is to help the user to become familiar with MS-DOS, the world's most widely used personal computer operating system. The Guide takes the non-technical computer user step by step through the commands which enable the effective and safe management of files, directories and disk security as well as providing an introduction to the way in which personal computers (PCs) are configured.

It is undoubtedly the case that users are becoming increasingly isolated from the actual MS-DOS command line. Computers are set up on behalf of users so that they can access programs via menus, or through the much more user-friendly Windows environment. Nevertheless, it has been found that a secure basic familiarity with the underlying DOS structure and its commands gives people far more confidence to deal effectively with the day-to-day running of their PCs, and even more importantly, to sort out some of the problems associated with file and disk management.

It is especially true that those who are taking computer studies courses at GCSE, A level or BTEC, or other courses that include computing, will gain valuable insights into the workings of computers by having a thorough familiarisation with the operating system.

One of the difficulties of producing a simple, practical guide to MS-DOS is the variety both of different hardware configurations and also of the variations in the way MS-DOS itself can be configured. The author has assumed that users of MS-DOS 5 and 6 will have access to a computer with a hard disk and at least one floppy disk drive (referred to in the text as **drive C** and **drive A** respectively).

Since MS-DOS was released in 1981 at the time IBM launched its first Personal Computer, it has been a constant battle to stay within sight of the rapid developments in hardware. Microsoft issued ten upgrades of the software in the decade up to the release of the greatly improved MS-DOS version 5 in 1991.

The power of the modern PC and the enormous increases in memory and disk capacity have meant that optimisation and detailed configuration have become increasingly technical. The intricacies of memory management and advanced hard disk organisation are beyond the scope of this Training Guide. Rather, it aims to give a thorough grounding in file and basic disk management, together with an introduction to configuration so that minor modifications can be made without endangering the security of the system.

Background to MS-DOS

MS-DOS stands for Microsoft Disk Operating System. Microsoft is the American software company that produced these programs. The system is often referred to simply as 'DOS', which is also the generic name for any software company's Disk Operating System.

Software

There are two main types of software, **systems software** and **applications software**. Systems software, of which DOS is an example, manages the workings of the computer. Apart from DOS itself, systems software includes so-called utilties programs such as disk doctors and anti-virus programs and Graphical User Interface (GUI) programs like Windows. Applications software includes programs such as word processors, spreadsheets, accounts packages, and other software that performs some task not directly associated with the working of the computer itself. The operating system of a typical personal computer comes in two distinct parts, the **Disk Operating System** and the **BIOS**.

The BIOS

BIOS stands for Basic Input Output System and it has nothing at all to do with the BASIC programming language. The BIOS is supplied by the computer manufacturer along with the computer's hardware in a reserved part of memory called ROM, or read-only memory. The user has no access to this part of the system. The BIOS controls the low-level operation of the computer's input and output devices such as the keyboard and disk drives.

When you first switch on the power, programs in ROM also enable the computer to **boot up.** First the memory and peripherals (e.g. keyboard, printer) are checked. Next a search is made for the **system files,** starting with the floppy drive, then the hard disk, or possibly the file-server if the PC is connected to a network.

The BIOS is rather like the subconscious part of your brain that controls heart-rate, reflex activities, etc. You cannot communicate directly with the BIOS to override its automatic control of hardware functions any more than you can directly interfere with the signals that control your heart!

The Disk Operating System

The MS-DOS operating system provides the primary interface between you and your computer so that you can issue commands to set up the working environment, load and run applications programs, as well as managing files, disk organisation and other so-called housekeeping jobs.

The base level interface is the MS-DOS **command processor**. You have to type in a command according to the exact syntax of the MS-DOS command language. If the command processor recognises what you have typed as a valid command it will be executed; otherwise an error message such as **Bad command or filename** will appear. These error messages can be somewhat terse, and particularly for beginners, they seem far from user-friendly.

The screen-based interface

One of the features of MS-DOS 6 is that a number of utilities programs have been included. Disk compaction utilities such as **doublespace** and **antivirus** programs were formerly available only from other software manufacturers.

The new 'bundled' utilities differ from the older style DOS commands in that, instead of having a complicated command syntax to control the way the command works, a screen is displayed which offers the user guidance and choices within an interactive environment. Extensive on-line help is available when you press the **F1** key.

Many of the command-based tasks that you will learn about in this Guide can also be accomplished interactively through the even more user-friendly Windows Graphical User Interface (GUI) system.

Even so, it is often very much quicker to type in a single DOS command than to have to go through seemingly endless Windows menus and dialog boxes.

There is no doubt that Windows currently provides the best environment for many applications, from the screen-based utilities to word processing and desktop publishing packages. For managing files and disks, using Windows is rather like taking a sledgehammer to crack a nut.

What to do if a command won't work

If you follow the instructions in this Training Guide carefully and type in a command with scrupulous attention to detail and it doesn't work, it can be most perplexing! The reason for this frustrating situation is most probably because MS-DOS cannot find the command.

The most commonly used MS-DOS commands are loaded into memory when the computer is first switched on. These so-called **memory-resident** or **internal commands** are then accessible at any time they are required. Less frequently used commands are stored on disk in the form of programs called **external commands**.

An external command is loaded into memory only when the user types its name. Unless the computer has been configured correctly, the MS-DOS command processor will be unable to locate the program and the external command will fail to operate.

If you find that external commands like **tree, format** and **chkdsk** do not appear to work, then you will have to reconfigure MS-DOS so that the command processor can find them. This involves first locating the external commands yourself, then assigning the location to a system variable called **path**. To save having to repeat this procedure, the statement that assigns the path variable is usually placed in the **autoexec** program which runs every time the computer is switched on.

Although this is explained in detail in Tasks 22 and 26, at this stage it would be sensible to seek help from a more knowledgeable friend or colleague.

Using your keyboard with MS-DOS

The (Enter) key

Always press the (Enter) key when you have finished typing a command. This is used as a signal for DOS to begin processing the command.

Computer keys

Computers never use the lower-case letter l in place of the numeric character **1**. Be careful to differentiate between the number nought **0**, (zero) and the upper-case capital **O**. There are additional keys on the computer that have functions which are special both to DOS and to other programs you are likely to use.

Cursor control keys

The (Spacebar) moves the cursor one character at a time to the right. The Backspace key deletes characters as it moves the cursor to the left. The arrow keys are not normally used in DOS command processing, except in the new screen-based utilities in MS-DOS 6 like **Help**, **Anti-Virus** and **MSbackup**.

The (Ctrl) key located in the bottom left corner of the keyboard enables the transmission of special control codes to the processor. You must hold down the control key and give a quick press of another key as you would when using the shift key for a capital letter. You will see control key combinations printed in either of the forms: **Ctrl-Z** or (Ctrl) + **Z**

Function keys

Along the top of the keyboad is a group of special function keys labelled **F1** to **F12**. They can be programmed to do different tasks depending on the particular software package you are using. A common convention in many packages is that **F1** is the Help key. In MS-DOS, the function keys provide various short cuts. They are described in great detail in the **MS-DOS Manual**, but there seem to be few people who make full use of them. I have included some of the more useful ones in the list below.

Key **Explanation**

F1   access to **Help** only in the screen-based utilities.
F2 c repeats the last command up to the character (c) specified.
F3   repeats the last command completely.
F6   saves having to type **Ctrl-Z** which is the end-of-file character.

Acknowledgements

I would like to thank my publisher Pitman Publishing for their support, especially Shelley Couper for her advice and Elizabeth Tarrant for having all the best qualities an editor should possess.

I would also like to thank my colleague Brian Street of the University of Greenwich for his help when beta testing MS-DOS 6.

Finally I would like to thank Dr Rowan Mould of Richmond College for her generous and kind allowance of far more than my fair share of access to our home computer.

Trade marks

Unless otherwise acknowledged, all names of persons, companies and addresses in this book are purely fictitious and are for example only.

Microsoft, MS, MS-DOS, Windows Word and Excel are all registered trademarks of Microsoft Corporation.

Mirror, Undelete and Unformat are the property of Central Point Software Inc.

Apple is a registered trademark of Apple Corporation
Atari is a registered trademark of Atari Corporation
BBC is a registered trademark of the British Broadcasting Corporation
IBM is a registered trademark of International Business Machines Corporation
Lotus and 1-2-3 are registered trademarks of Lotus Development Corporation
Norton is a registered trademark of Symantec Corporation
WordPerfect is a registered trademark of WordPerfect Corporation

Typeset by the author using the Timeworks Desk Top Publisher

Getting started

Powering up

When you first switch on your computer, various system checks are made and messages will be displayed, often very briefly, telling you about the computer's configuration. Depending on the way the machine has been set up, you may automatically find yourself at the DOS prompt, Microsoft Windows, or even in a package such as a word processor.

The DOS prompt

When the computer is waiting for you to enter a DOS command it displays the DOS, or system prompt, e.g. C:\>

The so-called 'C prompt' tells you that the internal hard disk, usually referred to as **drive C,** is the current drive. The system prompt will vary according to the current drive, so don't be put off if your computer is displaying a DOS prompt similar to one of the examples below:

A>   B:\>   P:\DOS>   n:\userc12>

If your computer is not displaying a system prompt, this is because it has been made to jump straight into Windows, a software package, or a set of choices from a **menu.** In order to start learning DOS you need to exit from the **menu** or package. Most Windows software will have an **Exit** option under the pop-down **File** menu which is usually the first option on the **Menu Bar** at the top of the screen. You may have to go back several levels until you finally get out!

You cannot normally issue a DOS command when you are in a package such as a word processor or spreadsheet.

The system clock

Shortly after switching on, and depending on the way your system is behaving, the computer may be expecting you to reset the date and time. All IBM PC-compatible computers have an internal clock. In many cases it will be powered by a battery so that it will continue to work even when the computer is not switched on.

If there is no clock, or the battery is down, the default time and date will appear on the screen every time the computer is powered up. You will then be expected to enter the current date and time. This will be explained in the first Activity.

Please read through each Activity before entering the commands. If you have a problem, look ahead to the section headed Troubleshooting.

Section A
Simple commands

Task 1: Resetting the system clock
Task 2: Finding out the current version of MS-DOS
Task 3: Changing the current drive

Task 1	Resetting the system date and time

● To check that the system clock has been set correctly and to reset it
● To use the on-line help facility

Every time a file is created, edited or updated, DOS uses the computer's internal clock to record the time and date of this activity in the disk directory. It is easier to keep track of files that have been correctly dated.

Activity 1.1   Resetting the date

1   At the system prompt, TYPE the command **date** and PRESS (ENTER)

The computer will respond like this:

```
Current date is Tue 03-12-1993
Enter new date (dd-mm-yy):
```

2   TYPE in the date: **24-05-94** and PRESS (ENTER)

The numbers corresponding to the day-month-year are separated only by dashes.
Do not include any spaces when you enter dates or times. If you make a mistake you can press the backspace key and retype a character. The command is not processed until you press the (ENTER) key.

3   To check that you have reset the date correctly, do steps 1 and 2 again.

The new date will be displayed as in step 1 above for you to check. If you don't want to change it again, press the (ENTER) key to accept the date as displayed, otherwise type in a different date.

Activity 1.2 Practising the command

You can use the **date** command to discover the day of the week on which a future date will fall. For instance you could find out the day of your birthday in the year 2000, or the day when you will be 21, or even 40 perhaps!

1 TYPE the command **date** (ENTER)

2 TYPE in a future date, then PRESS (ENTER)

3 To see the full date displayed, TYPE **date** (ENTER) again.

4 When you've finished experimenting, please reset the date correctly to today's date.

Activity 1.3 Setting the time

1 At the DOS prompt TYPE the command **time** (ENTER)

   The computer displays the time in hours, minutes, seconds and tenths of a second:

   ```
   Current time is 12:17:12.34
   Enter new time:
   ```

2 DOS is waiting for you to TYPE in the time in 24 hour clock format, e.g. **10:30**

You need only enter the time in hours and minutes separated by the colon.
Always press the (ENTER) key when you have finished typing in data or commands.

3 TYPE the command **time** again so that the new time is displayed for you to check.

4 To accept the time as displayed, PRESS (ENTER) or TYPE in yet another time.

Don't forget to reset the date and time correctly before you finally quit the activity, otherwise wrong and confusing information may be recorded when files are updated.

Troubleshooting

Your computer may have been set up so that dates are displayed in American format: mm-dd-yy (month-day-year). In this case you would have to type in 24 May 1994 as 05-24-94.

If the error messages **Invalid time** or **Invalid date** appear, it is probably because you've made a mistake in the format. Perhaps you forgot the dash (minus sign) separating the parts of the date, or you didn't put a colon between the hours and minutes when setting the time.

Activity 1.4   Getting help

The **help** command is a feature of MS-DOS 5. Use **help** if you forget what commands are available or how to use them, e.g.

1   TYPE **help** (ENTER) to list the available DOS commands with a brief definition.

2   TYPE **help time** (ENTER) to get information about a particular command.

There is a shortcut method of getting help which is to include the **help switch '/ ?'** after the command, e.g. you could TYPE **date / ?**

Help in MS-DOS 6

Help has been further enhanced in MS-DOS 6. The commands can still be entered as described above, but the output is rather more sophisticated. Typing **help** (ENTER) gives you a table of contents from which you can select detailed information about the command you want. If you have a mouse you can point to the required command, then click. Using the keyboard, you press the initial letter of the command on which you want help. If the first command selected is not the one you want, continue pressing the same key until you access the required command.

Moving between help topics

When the information about the command is displayed, you can use the Up and Down arrow keys and the Page Up and Page Down keys to move about the text. Hold down the (Alt) key and press the following keys to move within **help**:

N to move to the Next topic
B to go Back to the previous topic
C to return to the Contents page
F to go to the File menu

Press the (Esc) key to return to the previous **help** level. To quit **help**, hold down the (Alt) key and press **F** for File, then **X** for exit, or use the mouse to point to the file menu and then select the exit option.

The (Enter) key

From now on I shall assume that you will remember to press the (ENTER) key after typing each command.

Task 2	# The current version of MS-DOS

● To ascertain the version of DOS installed on your computer

A number of versions of DOS have been released over the years and you need to be certain which one is currently running. When you purchase and install software you will need to specify the version of DOS that you are using.

Activity 2.1 Displaying the current version of DOS

The command **ver** displays the working version of DOS

1 TYPE **ver** (ENTER)

The computer should respond with the message:

MS-DOS Version 6.00 (or 5.00)

If you see a message like this:

IBM Personal Computer DOS Version 3.30

you will need to find a book that covers the older versions of MS-DOS.

Troubleshooting

Problems can arise, for instance, when users attempt to execute DOS commands from a floppy disk which has DOS programs copied from a computer which has an earlier version installed. The most common difficulties relate to formatting disks and restoring backup files.

Usually an error message will be displayed:

Incorrect DOS version

In April 1993 MS-DOS 6 was released. Microsoft has announced that this is to be the final version of the operating system. The majority of commands remain the same, some have minor upgrades and a number of important utilities have been added. Some of the advanced features are beyond the scope of this guide. Unless you are specifically warned, you can assume that the MS-DOS 5 example given will continue to work with MS-DOS 6.

| Task 3 | # Changing the current drive |

● This task will show you how to select and enable a disk drive

DOS assigns an identifying letter to each disk drive of your computer.
A so-called 'base level system' will normally have a single floppy disk drive
which is referred to as **drive A**. If there is another floppy disk drive it will be
called **drive B**. The internal hard disk is normally called **drive C**. If you are
working on a network you may come across other drive letters such as **N**.

When referring to a disk drive in the context of entering a DOS command, you
must always include the colon ':' immediately after the drive letter, e.g. **A:**

Activity 3.1   Changing to the floppy disk drive

On most systems the **default drive** will be **drive C** and this will also be the **current drive**.

If the system prompt is indicating that the current drive is indeed **drive C** you can try
changing to **drive A**. Make sure your practice disk is in the drive before you start.

1   TYPE **a:** [ENTER]

The prompt should change to **A>** or **A:\>**, depending on how it has been set up.

If you have a second floppy disk drive, try changing to **drive B:**

2   TYPE **b:** [ENTER]

The DOS prompt should change to **B>** or **B:\>** Note that drive letters, like all commands,
may be typed in lower case letters.

3   Finally, change back to **drive C** by TYPING **c:** [ENTER]

4   If you are working on a network you may like to see if you can change to other drives on
the server. Ask the network manager for a list of the drive letters that are available to you.

Troubleshooting

Even if you didn't have any problems with changing drives, you are bound to come across error messages sooner or later, so read through the following notes in any case. You will learn a lot by deliberately trying to make a mistake which causes one of the error messages below:

1 `Bad command or filename`

This error occurs when you type **A** or **A;** (semicolon) instead of **A:** (colon). DOS is very particular about the colon after the drive letter, but it does not mind whether you type commands in CAPITAL LETTERS or in lower-case letters.

2 `Invalid drive specification`

This message appears when you don't have a drive corresponding to the letter you typed. If you haven't yet seen this error message try changing to a drive called Q just to see what happens! The exception to this is when you attempt to change to a non-existent **B** drive so that you can copy one floppy disk to another.

`Insert diskette for drive B: and press any key when ready`

To change back again, you just type **A:**

3 `Not ready reading drive A`
   `Abort, Retry, Fail?`

This means that you have tried to change to an empty floppy disk drive. You could try putting a disk into the drive and then press **R** to retry, or you could press **F** for fail, in which case the temporary system prompt will appear:

`Current drive is no longer valid>`

In this case type **C:** ENTER to get back to where you started from.

4 `Sector not found error reading drive A`
   `Abort, Retry, Fail?`

You've loaded a disk that DOS cannot recognise. The error may be caused because:

1 The disk is new or has not been formatted.
2 The disk belongs to a non-IBM compatible computer such as an Atari.
3 The disk has become corrupted.

Press **F** for Fail and then type **C:** ENTER when you see the prompt:

`Current drive is no longer valid>`

Section B
The MS-DOS file store

| Task 4 | ## Investigating the DOS directory tree

● To learn how to find your way around the disk directory structure

When you use a software package such as a word processor or spreadsheet, both the programs and your own work are held in the computer's internal memory (RAM). When the computer is switched off, the contents of the RAM memory are lost. Programs and data that are required permanently are saved in the form of **files** in the MS-DOS file store which is held on disks. Disk and file management is the main task of a Disk Operating System.

Files are grouped together and stored in directories rather in the way that paper documents are categorized and put into folders, which are then placed in the various drawers of appropriate filing cabinets. The DOS directory structure is often visualised as an upside-down tree with the root at the top. The symbol for the root directory is the reverse oblique (backslash) \ symbol. A typical DOS file store will be organised into a tree structure looking something like this:

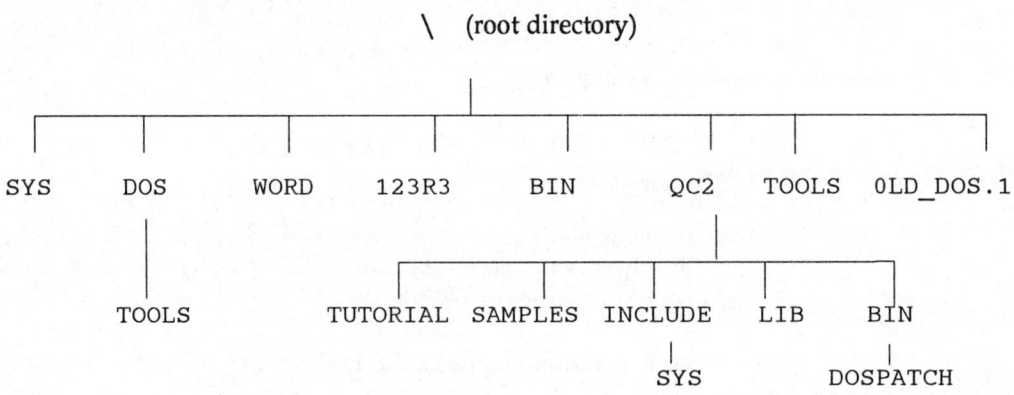

Activity 4.1   Investigating your directory tree

Make sure that the hard disk is the current drive.

1   TYPE **c:**

2   Next move to the root directory by TYPING **cd **

3   Then TYPE the command **tree**

NB Remember to press the (ENTER) key when you are ready to process a command.

The tree structure will be displayed vertically; compare the example below with the version on the previous page:

```
Directory PATH listing for Volume DISK1_VOL1
Volume Serial Number is 166A-8B9B
```

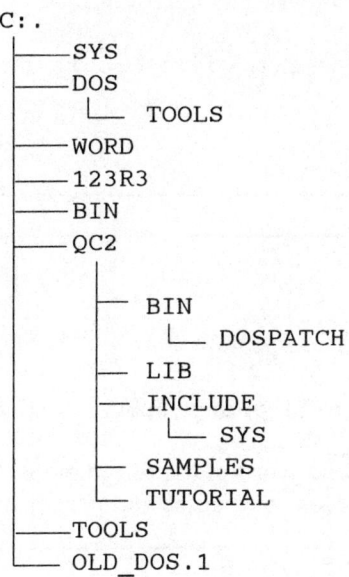

```
C:.
    ├────SYS
    ├───DOS
    │   └─  TOOLS
    ├───WORD
    ├──123R3
    ├──BIN
    ├──QC2
    │
    │          ┌─ BIN
    │          │  └─ DOSPATCH
    │          ├─ LIB
    │          ├─ INCLUDE
    │          │  └─ SYS
    │          ├─ SAMPLES
    │          └─ TUTORIAL
    ├───TOOLS
    └──  OLD_DOS.1
```

It would be useful to have a printout of your own directory tree for future reference.

4   If you have a local printer connected to your computer, TYPE the command **tree > prn**

The '>' symbol tells DOS to send the output of **tree** to the printer instead of to the screen.
prn is a device name used by DOS to identify the printer. If you are working on a network
you should see the network manager before attempting this step.

Troubleshooting

If the **tree** command did not work, it is probably because your computer has not been set up so that commands stored in one directory will work when you are in another directory or drive. See Task 22.

It is worth looking carefully at the output of the **tree** command and making a note of some of the directory names. What you see will depend on the software you have and where it has been installed on your hard disk. If you managed to get a printout of the display from **tree**, you should keep it.

Activity 4.2   To display the current directory

1   TYPE the command **cd**

If the current drive is your hard disk, and the current directory is the root directory, the output from the command **cd**, which stands for Current Directory, should look like this: C:\

The reverse oblique \ indicates that you are in the root directory of the drive indicated.

Your computer may have been set up to display the current directory within the prompt itself. If so your prompt will look like this: C:\>

otherwise you may see the default prompt: C>

Activity 4.3   Resetting the system prompt

1   First reset the prompt to the default by TYPING the command **prompt**

2   To display the current directory and path, TYPE the command **prompt pg**

Make sure you type a space between the two words. The second word of the command is called the command **parameter**. There is always a space between commands and parameter(s).

The pg parameter

The **pg** parameter consists of two strings: **$p** indicates the **path** and drive of the current directory; **$g** indicates the **greater than >** sign.

The path concept is explained more fully on the next page. A typical command prompt displaying a path might look like this:

C:\QC2\LIB>

Changing to other directories

If your exploration of the tree structure of your hard disk reveals that there are directories below the root directory, you can practise making one of them the current directory. I won't be able to tell you exactly what to press because I don't know the exact directory structure of your disk. You can easily remember the command **cd** because it stands for change directory.

The general form of the **cd** command is:

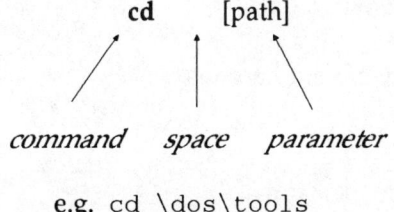

e.g. `cd \dos\tools`

(Don't forget the space between the command and the parameter(s).)

When a DOS command is given in its general form, **parameters** like `[path]` in square brackets are optional. To specify a parameter, you must leave out the brackets and substitute data of the type defined, like this:

`cd \cm\text`

\cm\text is an example of a **path**. It shows the path from the root directory \ to the subdirectory **text** via a directory named after my initials **cm**. Because the DOS directory tree on a large hard disk can be quite substantial some pathnames can be long, for instance: `\users\cm\text\letters`

Further practice

Now try changing to one of the directories that you noted down earlier when you used the **tree** command. If you get stuck, don't worry because a bit later on you will create a directory structure and then I can tell you exactly how to move around it.

Getting help

Don't forget that you can use the **help** command to get information about DOS commands. The definitions tend to be rather terse, but the facility is useful on those occasions when you do not have your Training Guide handy.

For information on the **cd** command, TYPE **help cd**

Using the directory command

● To list files in the current directory using the command **dir**

dir is probably the most widely used DOS command. Whenever you want to find out what files are on a particular disk, or are trying to locate a file, you will need to list the contents of a disk or directory.

Activity 5.1   Listing the root directory

First check that you are in the root directory of your hard disk.

1   At the DOS prompt, TYPE the commands:

   c:

   **cd **   (Remember to press the (ENTER) key after each command)

2   To list all the files in the root directory, TYPE **dir**

If there are many files present in the current directory the first few lines of the listing will probably disappear by scrolling off the top of the screen.

The **dir** command displays several pieces of information about each file as well as returning a count of the number of files present in the directory. It also tells you how much space (measured in bytes, or characters) is left on the disk. A typical directory listing will look something like this:

```
AUTOEXEC  BAT          249   24-09-90 2:40p
BACKUP    LOG          339   05-02-90 3:34p
PCTOOLS          <DIR>        22-02-90 7:34p
UTILS            <DIR>        27-10-90 2:10a
T         BAT          303   01-10-90 2:14p
SH_HISTO              13   29-07-92 5:33p
DEASE            <DIR>        03-02-91 7:05p
OLD_DOS   1      <DIR>        10-03-91 5:19p
WINA20    386          9349 13-12-90 4:09a
F         BAT          24    25-08-91 5:39p
25 file(s) 161713 bytes
           8175616 bytes free
```

Notice that there is about 8 Megabytes of free space remaining on the disk, which is enough to store approximately 8 million characters.

Activity 5.2 To list files in other directories

You can list files in directories other than the current directory by using two alternative methods:

1 Include the path of the other directory as a **parameter** to the **dir** command.

For instance, to list files in a directory called \DOS you would TYPE:

dir \dos

2 Change to the other directory to be listed, then list the files there.

This is a two stage procedure. TYPE:

cd \dos

dir

On the whole it is better to change to the directory that you want to list. This saves confusion in case you mistakenly list the current directory.

3 Now use the **cd** command to change to other directories on your hard disk, then use **dir** to list the files there.

Activity 5.3 Adding 'switches' to the dir command

The **dir** command can be refined by adding a number of **switches** which are separated from the command by the forward oblique / character.

1 When the list of files is too long to be displayed on the screen you can prevent the display from scrolling by adding the **/p** (pause) switch to the command:

dir /p

The **/p** switch instructs **dir** to display a single page at a time and then to pause while you read the information.

2 When you see the message: Strike a key when ready...

you should PRESS any key such as the (SPACE BAR) to continue the listing.

Notice that the output from **dir** is displayed in six columns, e.g.:

```
1           2     3       4       5           6
COMMAND   COM           46246   13-12-90   4:09a
BHS             <DIR>           08-05-92   9:30p
```

1 The main part of the filename
2 The filename type or **extension**
3 Shows whether the name belongs to a directory
4 The extent of the file in bytes (i.e. the number of characters it contains)
5 and 6 indicate the date and time the file was last updated or changed

Alternatively, the listing can be displayed using the 'wide format' switch: **/w**
The wide format display will look something like this:

```
C:\>dir /w
```

```
COMMAND.COM    [BHS]      DMDRVR.BIN   CONFIG.SYS    [SYS]
[DOS]          PARK.COM   SETUP.COM    [WORD]        [CM]
[BP]           [LOTUS]    [PITMAN]     DTREE.COM     [MEMO]
     15 file(s) 101713 bytes
     8175616 bytes free
```

With the wide format display you lose out on the amount of information, but more files can be displayed. The names of directories are enclosed in square brackets, like [PITMAN] which is a directory where I keep files relating to Pitman Publishing.

Activity 5.4 Using command parameters to list particular files

Suppose you want to display information about a particular file. Rather than having to scan through perhaps several screens of other files, you could include the filename as an optional **parameter** after the command. In Activity 3.3 you learned that a **parameter** is data, sometimes referred to as an object on which the command can operate.

1 To list only that file called **autoexec.bat**, you would TYPE:

dir autoexec.bat

If the file is present in the current directory you should get a display like this:

```
C:\>dir autoexec.bat
Volume in drive C: is HARD_DISK
Directory of C:\
AUTOEXEC BAT 249 24-09-91 2:40p
```

2 To list other files singly, SUBSTITUTE the full filename and its file type separated by the full stop, e.g.

dir config.sys

Summary: Command syntax or specification

The formal specification of a command is expressed in a statement written in **command syntax** which looks like this:

dir [path] [/s] [/w]

The command itself is printed in boldface type and must be typed in exactly as shown. The parameters are printed in normal typeface; each one is separated by a space. The square brackets tell you that certain words of the command represent optional parameters or switches. In the example above, the parameter [path] can include a single filename or a complete path such as \word\docs.

When you type a path, filename or switch, do not include the square brackets.

There are more **dir** switches for you to learn about in later activities.

To see an example of command syntax, TYPE **help dir**

Troubleshooting

Read this section even if everything went smoothly. Try making deliberate mistakes to see if you can get the error messages described below.

1 After you typed: **dir autoxec.bat**, you got the message:

    File not found

You misspelled the filename, or a file of that name does not exist in the current directory. There is normally a file called AUTOEXEC.BAT in the root directory.

If you were looking for information on the file CONFIG.SYS and you typed **dir config**, you should expect the **File not found** error message unless there is also a file called CONFIG without the extension .SYS

2 At the C:\> prompt, suppose you typed: dirautoexec.bat

You would see the error message: Bad command or filename

This is because you didn't leave a space between the command **dir** and the parameter **autoexec.bat**.

Task 6	# Looking for files

- To find particular files by using **dir** parameters and switches
- To learn more about DOS files
- To use the additional features of **dir** in MS-DOS 5 and 6

In previous activities, you have used **dir** to display a particular file's details. If you did not type the name correctly, the 'File not found' error message was returned. In real-life situations you will often be unable to remember the exact name of a file. You can use so-called **wildcard** characters to substitute for parts of a filename. Many filenames consist of common patterns or strings of characters and can be listed as a group.

The disk drive capacity of PCs is always increasing, so the **dir** command has been considerably enhanced in MS-DOS 5 and 6 to make it easier to search rapidly through many directories.

There are now so many options available for **dir** that you can't possibly remember them all. Don't forget that you can type **help dir** to get a full command specification which includes a list of all the option switches.

Hopefully you will be working on a computer with a good many directories and files, otherwise some of the following exercises will be rather academic.

Activity 6.1 Looking for groups of files

All files beginning with a particular letter or group of letters can be found and listed by substituting the star * **wildcard** character in place of the unspecified characters.

1 If you are not already in the root directory of the hard disk, TYPE the commands:

   c:
   **cd **

2 To search the root directories for any files whose names begin with the three letters **com** , you should TYPE:

   dir com*.*

   An instructor would say this aloud to you like this: 'D I R space com star dot star'.

Searching the directory tree using the /s switch

To look for all instances of files beginning with a three-letter pattern or string of characters, you would need to look further than the root directory. The **/s** switch placed at the end of the **dir** command instructs DOS to search all subdirectories below the current directory for files which begin with the string specified in the parameter.

1 So, to find and locate all those files beginning with the string **com**, you would TYPE:

   dir com*.* /s

2 To look for filenames that begin with the letter **A** or with the string **WIN**, TYPE:

   dir a*.* /s

   dir win*.* /s

3 Continue to practise by looking for files beginning with other single letters or strings of letters. If you have any problems it will probably be because you have left out the space between **dir** and the **parameter**. Say to yourself:

   'D I R space win star dot star slash s'.

Interpreting the listings

These useful directory listings help you to locate file(s) anywhere in the MS-DOS file store. They also show you where there are duplicate, and possibly unwanted, versions of the same file and also the exact directory where the files are located. This will be helpful later when you will learn how to tidy up a disk.

Troubleshooting

Suppose you typed **dir com   *.* /s**, you would have seen the error message:

```
too many parameters - *.*
```

This is because you left a space between the string you're searching for, and the wildcard combination. A space is required between the command and its parameter, not in the middle of a parameter.

Rules about filenames

Before you can use some of the other features of **dir** you need to know a little more about files and filenames. In Activity 3.2 you learned that DOS filenames are made of two parts, separated by a full stop, or 'dot'. For instance:

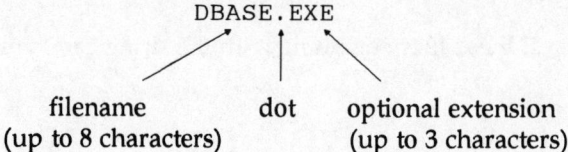

DBASE.EXE

| | filename | dot | optional extension |
| | (up to 8 characters) | | (up to 3 characters) |

Filenames can be made of any combinations of the letters A-Z, the numbers 0-9, and certain other characters but not " : / ? *

Valid filenames can be in CAPITALS or lower-case letters, e.g.:

```
ACCOUNTS.DAT  config.sys  MEMO12  1.bat  TEMP.$$$
```

These filenames would not be allowed:

ACCOUNTS.DATA	extension too long
accounting.1	filename too long
MEMO/jdh	invalid character /

The optional extension is a useful way of telling what sort of file you're dealing with. Here are some typical conventions:

Extension	Stands for	Meaning
COM	COMMAND	binary code program or command
EXE	EXECUTABLE	program
BAT	BATCH	program made up of DOS commands
SYS	SYSTEM	system or device configuration
BAS	BASIC	program written in BASIC
PRG	PROGRAM	program written in dBASE
OVL	OVERLAY	subprograms
DOC	DOCUMENT	word processor or text file
DAT	DATA	data file
WKS	WORKSHEET	spreadsheet data file
PIC	PICTURE	graphics file
FNT	FONT	special typeface
ASC	ASCII	file of readable characters
LST	LIST	output or list from a command or report
PRN	PRINT	text sent to a file instead of to the printer

Activity 6.3   Listing files with the same extension

It is often very useful to be able to list all the files that share the same extension.

1   Check that you are in the root directory of the hard-disk; TYPE the commands:

   c:
   **cd **

2   To list all command files that end in **.com** you should TYPE:

   dir *.com /s   (D I R space star dot com slash s)

   Example output:

   ```
   Volume in drive C is HARD-DISK
   Directory of C:\
   BTREE COM 3416 12-12-90  8:05a        (The three files listed are
   BASIC COM 9806 05-23-91 10:05a         all of COMMAND file type)
   ADMIN COM 1650 12-08-93  7:06p
         3 File(s) 323584 bytes free
   ```

3   To find all files ending in **.exe** TYPE:

   dir *.exe /s

4   To list all the **system** files TYPE the command: **dir *.sys**

Other groups of files to look for might end in: **.wks .dat .bat .doc**

Troubleshooting

Make sure you do not leave out the space between the command **dir** and its parameters. There are **never** any spaces inside a filename, **nor** between a switch and its letter, so the filenames **cm .doc** and **memo. txt** are both incorrect as is **/ s**.

Take care not to leave out the dot that separates the two parts of the filename. DOS itself does not display the dot in full directory listings, which can be confusing.

Activity 6.4 The question mark ? wildcard

The question mark ? is another **wildcard** character which can be used in place of a single character occupying a particular position in the filename.

1   To display a wide listing of all files with extensions that end with the two letters **at** you would TYPE:

dir *.?at /s /w

e.g. `ACCOUNTS.DAT    AUTOEXEC.BAT    NOMINAL.DAT    SPEED.PAT`

2   Now try looking for files whose extensions start with the letters **wk**, such as

wks, wk1, wk2.

Hint: substitute the **?** **wildcard** in place of the last character of the extension.

When to use the question mark ? wildcard

The ? wildcard is very useful when you are looking for files that contain coded numbers or patterns of characters within the filename.

For instance the Typographica collection of **fonts** (or typefaces) has the general file format **tttpppss.eee** where **ttt** is a three letter typeface code like FUT for Futura; **ppp** is the point size in the range 001 to 999; **ss** is the style code, for instance, BD for **bold,** or IT for *Italic.* The file extension **eee** tells you which device the font is for, e.g. a VGA screen.

Thus the file with the name **FUT012BD.VGA** stores the data needed to display FUTURA 12 point boldface on a VGA screen. If you want to list all the different 12 point fonts you'd use the combination **dir ???012??.***

On the other hand to list all the Italic fonts of any point size and for any device, you would type: **dir ??????it.***

Activity 6.5 Further practice

1   List all files with the extensions .ME .DOC .STY (three separate jobs)
2   List all files beginning with W
3   List all files whose second letter is E
4   List all files whose extension ends with a T

If you get really stuck, there are some suggested answers on the next page.

Ordered directory listings: the /o switch

The **/o** switch determines the order in which files are listed by **dir**. It can be followed by one of five pairs of secondary switches which determine the sort order. By itself, **/o** lists directories first, then filenames in alphabetical order. Be careful to use the letter 'o' and not zero '0'.

Switch	Meaning
/on	names are displayed alphabetically including directories
/o-n	names, including directories, displayed in reverse order (Z-A)
/oe	extension order
/o-e	extension order, reversed
/od	date and time order, oldest first
/o-d	date and time order, most recent first
/os	size order, smallest first
/o-s	size order, largest first
/og	groups directories first (same as /o)
/o-g	groups directories last

Notice that the minus sign negates the normal function of the secondary switch. The most useful secondary switch combinations are **oe** and **od** because listing files together by type and by date order respectively is very helpful.

When combining switches, each switch must be preceded by the forward oblique **/** symbol, except for secondary switches.

Suggested answers to Activity 6.5

Don't forget to include the **/s** switch if you want to search all subdirectories for the file group specified in the parameter.

1 **dir *.me /s**
  dir *.doc /s
  dir *.sty /s

2 **dir w*.* /s**

3 **dir ?e*.* /s**

4 **dir *.??t /s**

File attributes

In addition to rules about the number and type of characters that can be used to make a filename, files have other features called **attributes**, each of which has a pair of secondary directory switches associated with it. Use **help dir** for a full list of options.

Switch	Attribute
/ah	hidden file
/a-h	not hidden
/as	a DOS system file
/a-s	not a system file
/ad	directories listed only
/a-d	not directories, i.e. files only
/aa	files ready for archiving or back-up
/a-a	files unchanged since last back-up
/ar	read-only files, can't be updated or deleted
/a-r	not read-only, can be updated or deleted

The most often used combination is probably **/ad**, because you often want a list of directories only. The archive switches are also useful if you are organised about making regular backups, see Section D, Disks and Security.

Activity 6.7   Looking at file attributes with the /a switch

1   Change to a directory where there are plenty of files to list.

2   Now try some of the **/a** combinations on their own and with other **dir** switches.

Here are a couple of examples to start you off:

dir /ar
dir /ad /s

The /c switch, a MS-DOS 6 upgrade

Yet another switch has been added to **dir** in MS-DOS 6. The /c switch displays
the compression ratio of files that have been squashed up so as to take up less
space on the hard disk. **File compression** is the technique used by the MS-DOS
doublespace utility which claims to double the storage capacity of disk drives.
The trade off is that certain software, particularly databases, run rather more
slowly. Unless the doublespace utility has been installed on your machine, the /c
switch is redundant.

● To create your own subdirectories and to move about the tree structure

You will create your own branch of the directory tree structure below the root directory. So as to minimise the risk of causing problems with your hard disk **you are strongly advised to use your practice disk** for these exercises.

This is the directory structure you are about to make:

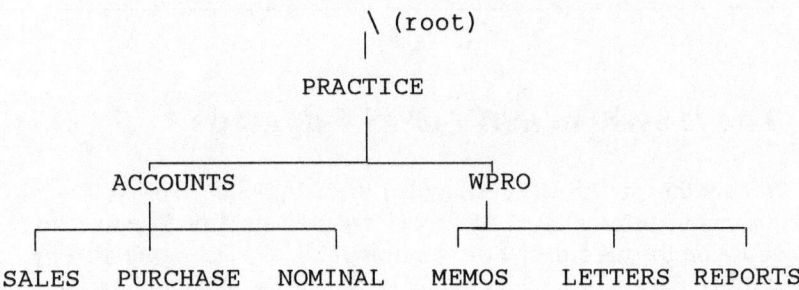

The two branches of the tree are to be set up so that an accounts package could be installed in **\practice\accounts**. The data files relating to the **sales, purchase** and **nominal** ledgers would then be stored in their respective directories at the next level. The other branch of the tree is to be prepared for the installation of a word processing package in the directory **wpro**. Documents can be stored in the directories **memos, letters** and **reports**.

Activity 7.1   Making new directories with the md command

Make sure that you have your practice disk in **drive A.**

1   The root directory of **drive A** should be the current directory:

a:
**cd **

2   To make the directory called **practice**, TYPE:

md practice

3   Check that this new directory has been made correctly by listing it:

dir practice

e.g. PRACTICE<DIR> 15-10-93 10.31a

Activity 7.2   Creating a new directory

To make a new directory at a lower level you must be in the parent directory.

1   To make the directories ACCOUNTS and WPRO you must first change to their parent directory which will be PRACTICE:

cd practice

If the DOS prompt has been set to show the path, it should look like this:

```
A:\PRACTICE>
```

But you can always display the current directory and path by typing **cd**

2   Now you can make two more directories: ACCOUNTS and WPRO

TYPE the commands:

md accounts
md wpro

3   Check that all has gone to plan by typing **dir**

The display should look like this:

```
Directory of A:\PRACTICE
  .          <DIR> 11-03-93 11:34a
  ..         <DIR> 11-03-93 11:34a
ACCOUNTS  <DIR> 15-05-93 10:35a
WPRO      <DIR> 15-05-93 10:35a
```

The directory PRACTICE now contains four subdirectories, the two you just made, and two strange ones, **dot** and **dot dot**.

Dot (.) indicates that it is possible to create child or subdirectories below the current directory. **Dot dot** (..) indicates that there is a parent directory above.

Activity 7.3 Continuing the branch of the tree below ACCOUNTS

You will now make the directories for the SALES, PURCHASE and NOMINAL ledger files. Remember that they are created below their parent directory, ACCOUNTS.

1 To make ACCOUNTS the current directory, TYPE **cd accounts**

The prompt should now display the path:

A:\PRACTICE\ACCOUNTS>

2 To make the new directories, TYPE the commands:

md sales
md purchase
md nominal

3 Check that the directories have been created by typing **dir**

Activity 7.4 Creating the WPRO branch of the tree

To set up the WPRO branch of the tree, you must first change to the WPRO parent directory. You can do this in either of these two ways:

1 By including the full path of the WPRO directory as the command parameter:

cd \practice\wpro

2 By dropping back to the common parent directory before changing to the required directory. To do this you TYPE the two commands:

cd ..
cd wpro

cd 'dot dot' takes you back one level at a time.
These two steps can be combined into one: **cd ..\wpro**

3 Once you're in the WPRO directory you can make the subdirectories MEMOS, LETTERS and REPORTS at the next level below. To make the first subdirectory, TYPE:

md memos

4 Using the example above, make the new subdirectories for LETTERS and REPORTS. If you get stuck, look again at Activity 7.3, step 2 at the top of the page.

5 Use **dir** to check that the directories have been created correctly.

Activity 7.5   Displaying your new directory structure

1   To display the tree stucture of drive **A** starting from the root directory, TYPE:

**tree **

The oblique **** parameter instructs **tree** to start scanning from the root directory, otherwise it will display the structure commencing at the current directory.

Troubleshooting

If you find that **tree** does not work and you get the error message:

`Bad command or filename`

it is because your computer has not been set up correctly. Except for **tree**, all the commands you have met so far have been so-called **internal commands**, that is, they are loaded into memory when the computer boots up and they remain in memory until the session is over and you switch off the power.

The **tree** command is one of the DOS **external commands** which is stored as a **.com** file usually in the \ DOS directory. Unless the computer has been configured so that there is always a path to the \ DOS directory, an external command such as **tree** will not work outside its home directory and drive. How to set and reset the path is covered in detail in Task 22.

To get round the problem for now, you could change to the **C drive**, make DOS the current directory, then include the **A drive** as the command parameter. To do this you need to TYPE the following commands:

c:
cd \dos
tree a:

If it still doesn't work, then presumably the **tree** command is located somewhere other than the \ DOS directory, if indeed there is one on your computer! In this case you need to look for **tree**, so use **dir** with the **/s** switch.

To search all directories below the root directory of the **C drive**, TYPE:

dir c:\tree.com /s

When you find it, move to the directory where it belongs, and TYPE:

tree a:

Activity 7.6   Moving to the lowest branch

If you've successfully finished building the WPRO branch of the tree you can make LETTERS
the current directory.

1   Check that your DOS **prompt** is indicating the path `A:\PRACTICE\WPRO>`

2   Now TYPE the command:

cd letters

The prompt should now display the complete path from the root to LETTERS:

`A:\PRACTICE\WPRO\LETTERS>`

Troubleshooting

If this does not happen according to plan, it could be because:

1   You were not in the parent directory when you typed **cd letters**.
In this case you would have to TYPE the complete path as the parameter:

cd \practice\wpro\letters

2   You have failed to make the subdirectory LETTERS or it is in the wrong
place on your tree. Have a critical look at your tree structure with **tree **

Activity 7.7   Moving to other directories

To help you understand this activity, refer to the tree diagram on page 22.
Assuming that the **prompt** is still displaying the path as shown below:

`A:\PRACTICE\WPRO\LETTERS>`

1   Use the **cd ..** combination to move to the sister directories MEMOS
and then REPORTS, like this:

cd ..\memos

2   Practise these moves, starting from the root directory:

TYPE **cd **

To go directly to WPRO, TYPE **cd practice\wpro**

Then move to NOMINAL, by TYPING **cd ..\accounts\nominal**

Activity 7.8   Further practice

Try working out these moves for yourself; it's a good idea to have the tree diagram handy.

1   Return to PRACTICE.

2   Go to WPRO.

3   Go to SALES.

4   Drop back to the parent of SALES.

5   Return directly to the root.

6   You could set up another branch of the tree below PRACTICE to store files belonging to a database that you might be about to create. The database programs themselves could live in a directory called RDBMS (Relational Database Management System). This will be a sister directory of WPRO and ACCOUNTS. Below this should be subdirectories that will store the actual database files relating to STAFF, CLIENTS and MAILSHOT.

7   When you have finished, display your work and, if possible, send the result to the printer.

To do this you would TYPE **tree \ >prn**

Keep your practice disk safe

You will need to use the directory structures you have created for later exercises.

Floppy disks should be kept flat and returned to their protective sleeves, especially if they are the more vulnerable 5.25 inch disks. Avoid touching the exposed parts of a disk. Always write on labels before you stick them on. Floppy disks should not be left in direct sunlight, or placed near a magnetic field, such as on top of a television set nor even the VDU screen you are looking at now! Put them away safely in a disk box, which itself should be kept in a drawer or filing cabinet.

Displaying text files

- To display the contents of a text file
- To consolidate the commands covered so far

So far you have used the commands **dir** and **tree** to look at information about files. You will now learn how to display the contents of a file. Users who don't know these tricks have to load a word processor just to look at a simple text file!

Activity 8.1   Displaying a file using the command 'type'

1   Make sure that the **prompt** is showing that the current drive and directory is C\>

If you're not there already, TYPE

c:
**cd **

Text files can be displayed by the command **type** followed by the filename:

type [filename.ext]

2   Do not enter the words and brackets '[filename.ext]' literally. You have to SUBSTITUTE the full name(s) of the file(s) you want to read, like this:

type autoexec.bat

Autoexec.bat contains a number of DOS commands that are automatically executed whenever the computer is first switched on or re-booted. It is dealt with in more detail later in Task 25.

Displaying long files

If the file is longer than 24 lines, the display will scroll up the screen and the first lines of the file will vanish. If your reactions are quick, you can suspend scrolling by pressing the (Pause) key, or hold down the (Ctrl) key and press **S**. Press any key to restart the display.

You can use **more** to display longer files one page at a time. **More** will prompt you to press a key when you are ready to move on to the next page.

To use **more** you would type **more<[filename]** e.g. `more<readme.txt`

More is a special command called a **filter** which processes the output of a command or file. The '<' sign tells DOS to **redirect** the specified file through the **more** filter.

Troubleshooting

The display consists of seemingly meaningless characters

Only text files, or data files in standard ASCII character format can be reliably displayed using **type** or **more**. If you try to read a program file, the screen will be filled with garbage, the machine will beep at you and the computer will probably 'hang up' on you as well! ASCII stands for American Standard for Character and Information Interchange. It defines the binary codes that represent human-readable characters for use in computers and communications devices. Thus a so-called ASCII file contains standard characters that can be read into most word processors or other common software packages.

.DOC files, though basically in ASCII format, may include word processing formatting characters which can give unpredictable results. Files with no extensions can usually be displayed using **type**, and files with README in the name are an invitation to do so!

Files ending in .COM and .EXE may not be **typed**, because they consist mainly of binary coded instructions to the processor or CPU. The **type** command attempts to convert them to their ASCII character equivalents, and the result is the confusing garbage you see if you try to use **type** to read a command file.

What to do if the computer hangs up

If nothing seems to happen when you press a key several times, it could be that the processor has 'hung'. If there are no signs of disk activity, you should try to **reboot** the computer. You can perform what is called a **warm boot** by leaving the power switched on. Press the ⟨RESET⟩ button, or hold the ⟨Ctrl⟩ and ⟨Alt⟩ keys down with the forefingers of the left hand and press the ⟨Del⟩ key on the extreme bottom right of the keyboard.

If these measures fail to work you will have to do a **cold boot** which means switching off the power. Wait until no more disk noise can be heard before you switch the power back on. **NB reboot** destroys the contents of working memory.

Activity 8.2 Looking for more files to inspect

Use the **dir** command with the **/s** switch (subdirectory search) to find suitable files to type.

As a general rule, you should get a readable display from files ending in:

```
.bat .sys .txt .asc .msg .prg .pas .c
```

The last two examples are PASCAL and C program files. You might like to try **type** or **more<** with an executable file ending in .COM or .EXE just to see what happens.

Section C
Managing files

Task 9: Copying files between directories and drives
Task 10: Copying files between other devices
Task 11: Deleting files
Task 12: Removing directories
Task 13: Renaming files and directories

This section will show you how to maintain files and directories simply and effectively. You should get into the habit of making regular backup copies of working files. Sooner or later every computer user wishes they had taken the trouble to do this. Equally important is being confident enough to erase unwanted files so that disks do not become clogged with redundant information.

| Task 9 |

Copying and moving files between directories and drives

● To copy files from one drive to another
● To use the wild characters to copy groups of files
● To move files using the new MS-DOS 6 command **move**

Files can be copied from one directory to another on a single disk drive, or from one drive to another. They can be copied one at a time or as a group by selecting their names using the wildcards * and ?.

Copying from device to device might involve file transfers between the hard disk and a floppy disk, or from an input device such as the keyboard directly to a disk file. Files can also be copied from a disk drive to a printer or other output device such as a modem or even a fax machine.

All these activities can be performed by using the **copy** command which is an **internal command,** that is, it becomes memory resident whenever the computer is booted up and DOS is loaded.

So that you do not create duplicate files all over your hard disk, you will need to use your practice disk for these exercises. If you have not yet made the directories according to the instructions in Task 7, please do them before commencing the following activities.

Activity 9.1   Copying files from the hard disk to a floppy disk

First you will copy some files to the root directory of your practice disk.

1   Put your practice disk into **drive A** and log into the root directory by TYPING:

   a:
   **cd **

I am assuming that there are some suitable source files in the root directory of your **C drive**. You don't want to copy too many, otherwise you'll run out of disk space on the target drive.

Because the files in the root directory will no doubt be mixed up with a lot of directories, you can use **dir** with the 'minus directories' file attribute switch **/a-d** to list them.

2   List files only in the root directory of **drive C** by TYPING:

   dir c:\ /a-d

If fewer than about a dozen filenames are listed, you can copy all of them in one operation by doing step 3 below, otherwise go straight on to Activity 9.2.

3   To copy all the files from the root directory of **C** to the current directory, TYPE:

   copy c:

Notice that **copy**, unlike **dir**, processes only files and not directories.

4   Check that the files have indeed been copied by TYPING **dir**

Activity 9.2   Copying selected files

Do this activity even if you did step 3 of Activity 9.1. You should be in the root directory of **A**.

1   Begin by copying the single file **autoexec.bat** by TYPING **copy c:\autoexec.bat**

   If the command works correctly, you will see the message:

   `1 File(s) copied`

2   Using the * wildcard, copy any other files ending in **.bat** by TYPING:

   copy c:*.bat

3   Copy any system files from the root directory of C by TYPING:

   copy c:*.sys

The basic syntax of the COPY command

    copy source [destination]

Notice that the first parameter, which is not within square brackets, is mandatory, that is to say, you **must** specify the source. You can substitute any combination of files, directories and devices into both the source and destination parameters, e.g.:

copy a:\ b:** copies all files from the root directory of **drive A to the root directory of **drive B.**

copy \dos*.com copies all the files with the extension **.com** from the DOS directory of the current drive to the default (i.e. current) directory because no second **target** parameter was specified.

copy \dos*.com a:** copies the same group of source files to the target which is the root directory of **drive A.

In the last two examples, since no drive was specified within the source parameter, you should assume that the source directory \DOS is located on the **current drive.**

Creating more practice files

In order to make the next exercises more realistic you need to make some entirely new files by redirecting the output of **dir** to some practice files.

Change to root directory of **drive A** and TYPE the following commands:

dir >ex1.lst   the extension **.lst** is to tell you that the file contains a listing
dir >ex2.lst   NB the first letter of the extension **.lst** is **L** not **1**
dir >ex1.dir   an alternative extension is **.dir**
dir >ex2.dir

Continue like this up to **ex5**, so as to make a good few example files.

The **>** symbol tells DOS to **redirect** the output of **dir** to the specified file.

Activity 9.3 Copying files between directories on the same disk drive

You may find it helpful to refer to the tree diagram on page 22 when doing the following activities.

1 To copy a file from the current directory to the directory called **practice** you TYPE:

copy   autoexec.bat   \practice

Be careful to separate each part of the command with a space. If an error message appears the chances are that you left out one of the spaces between the parameters.

2 To check that the file has been copied correctly, TYPE **dir \practice**

Now you can copy the files you made on page 34 when you redirected the output from **dir**. The wildcards * and ? can be used to copy a group of files to another directory.

3 TYPE the following commands:

copy   *.lst   \practice

copy   ex?.dir   \practice

dir   \practice

Activity 9.4 Copying files further down the tree

Before you start this Activity, make sure that you are in the root directory of **drive A**.

Suppose you need to copy all the files in the root directory to the ACCOUNTS subdirectory which is below \PRACTICE.

1 To do this TYPE **copy   *.*   \practice\accounts**

Depending on the number of files on your disk, DOS should respond like this:

```
10 File(s) copied
```

2 Now see what happens when you TYPE: **copy   *.*   \accounts**

You should see the response:

```
1 File(s) copied
```

This experiment illustrates how careful you must be to substitute the complete path of the destination directory you want to copy to.

The destination directory ACCOUNTS is below PRACTICE, not below the root directory. The command **copy *.* \accounts** instructs DOS to copy all files to a destination directory or file immediately below the root directory. Since there is no directory called ACCOUNTS below the root directory (it's below **\practice**), DOS opens a file called **accounts** and copies everything into this one file. That's why you see the message:

```
1 File(s) copied.
```

Complete the exercise by checking that there is now both a directory and a file called ACCOUNTS.

3 TYPE **dir accounts /s**

```
ACCOUNTS 9761 08-30-92 3:57p
1 file(s) 9761 bytes

Directory of A:\PRACTICE
ACCOUNTS <DIR> 08-30-92 3:56p 1 file(s) 0 bytes

Total files listed: 2 file(s) 0 bytes
```

If you intended to copy a group of files and DOS tells you that only one file has been copied, take care. The chances are that you have not properly specified the destination path.

Activity 9.5   Copying files to the current directory

1 Make the subdirectory WPRO the current directory by TYPING **cd \practice\wpro**

2 Now copy all the files ending in **.bat** from the root directory by typing **copy *.bat**

Because you did not include the destination parameter, the files should have been copied to the current directory.

3 Check this by examining the output from **dir**

4 Now make ACCOUNTS the current directory. Try to work this out for yourself by following the example in step 1.

5 COPY all the files in WPRO to the current directory: **copy \wpro**

6 Finally copy all the files from the \PRACTICE directory to the SALES directory.

Look carefully at the tree diagram on page 22 before attempting this.

The new MS-DOS 6 command 'move'

When you wanted to move a file from one directory to another, the procedure was to copy the file to the new location, then to delete the old file from the original directory. Users often omitted to delete the old file, and this was one of many ways in which disks got clogged with duplicated and otherwise unwanted files. If you have MS-DOS 6 you can easily move a file to a new location. **Move** can also be used to rename directories. See Task 13.

Activity 9.6   Using the move command (MS-DOS 6)

To move all the files ending in **.bat** from the WPRO directory back to the PRACTICE directory, first change directory to WPRO as you did in Activity 9.5. Then:

1   TYPE **move *.bat \practice**

You should see command output looking like this:

```
a:\autoexec.bat     => a:\practice\autoexec.bat [ok]
a:\menu.bat         => a:\practice\menu.bat [ok]
```

2   Check that the source files are no longer in the source directory WPRO and are now located in the PRACTICE directory. TYPE:

dir *.bat

dir \practice*.bat

3   Files that cannot be matched using wildcards can be moved by including them in a list separated by commas. Do not put a comma before the target directory, e.g.

move memo.txt, letter.doc, cv.doc \personal

Activity 9.7   Taking stock

Now that you have copied and moved files to the various directories on your practice disk, you can use the full power of the **tree** command to list both the directories and their contents.

1   Include the **/f** switch to generate a file listing within the **tree** display by TYPING:

tree a:\ /f

2   Keep your disk safely because you will need it again in Task 11, where you will learn how to tidy it up by deleting files safely.

Task 10   Copying files between devices

- To learn how to copy data between different peripheral devices
- To use **copy** to add files together to make a master file

The **peripheral** devices of a personal computer system consist of such hardware as the keyboard, the Visual Display Unit (VDU), printers, disk and tape drive units, whether fitted internally or externally.

The peripheral devices enable the input, output and permanent storage of data which is processed in the CPU (central processing unit), or microprocessor. The combination of VDU and keyboard at which you are working is an I/O (Input/Output) device called the **console**. In MS-DOS command syntax, **console** is abbreviated to **con.**

You can therefore use the **copy** command to copy a stream of characters directly between the console and a disk file in either direction. DOS can regard the console either as a source or a destination depending on the context of the command.

Activity 10.1   Copying from the keyboard directly to a disk file

Please read through the activity before you start to enter a command.

1   Make sure that you are in the root directory of your practice disk in **drive A.**

2   To copy a stream of characters from the console to a file called **ex10.txt**, TYPE:

    copy con ex10.txt (ENTER)

The cursor will move down to the next line. You will then type in the example text below, pressing the (ENTER) key at the end of every line, including the blank lines.

3   TYPE in the text as shown in boldface below:

This is a file called ex10.txt. It will contain the text I am typing now.

It was created by copying a stream of characters from the keyboard, which is a standard I/O device called con (short for console).

The process is terminated by the end-of-file character Ctrl-Z

After sending the end-of-file (EOF) character, the standard message will be displayed: 1 File(s) copied

Now HOLD down the (Ctrl) key, then PRESS **Z** (ENTER)

The command **copy con [filename]** is a simple but effective way of creating a short text file. If you make a mistake, and you notice it before you get to the end of the line, you can make a correction by using the backspace delete key. You cannot move the cursor up the screen to edit a previous line because you are not in a screen editor or word processor. You are simply copying a stream of characters one line at a time from one device to another.

If your function keys are set up for MS-DOS, you can press the [F6] function key to get the EOF character.

Activity 10.3 Creating your own simple text file

1 Make a text file containing a short message using **copy con [filename]**
You must think up your own filename and it should have the extension **.msg**
which normally identifies files of that sort, like this example:

copy con jane.msg

Remember to PRESS the [ENTER] key at the end of each line. To leave blank lines in the text, PRESS the [ENTER] key as many times as you require. To end the file, PRESS the [F6] function key, or HOLD down the [Ctrl] key and PRESS **Z** [ENTER]

2 Display the file using the **type** command, e.g.:

type jane.msg

Activity 10.4 Copying to a standard output device

You will need a local printer to able to do steps 1 to 3 of this activity. If the printer is connected to the usual parallel port at the back of the computer, DOS will address it by the device name **prn** or **lpt1**. If the printer is connected to the serial port it will probably be addressed as **com1**.

1   To copy the text of the file **ex10.txt** to the printer, TYPE **copy ex10.txt prn**

2   Copy the message file you made in Activity 10.2, e.g. TYPE **copy jane.msg lpt1**

3   TYPE the command **dir c:\read*.* /s** to locate any files on your hard disk with names like **read.me** or **readme.txt**.

4   Select a file that does not look too large and copy it to the printer, for example:

    copy c:\user\readme.txt prn

If you do not have a local printer you can still do the next step. Remember that the console is a combination of keyboard and VDU. It is therefore possible to copy a file to the console.

5   TYPE the command **copy ex10.txt con**

The effect is similar to the command **type ex10.txt**. As you learn more about DOS you will discover that there is often more than one way to do something. If you are printerless you could go back and practise steps 1 to 3, substituting **con** for each occurrence of **prn.**

Activity 10.5 Printing an envelope or address label

1   Feed an envelope into the printer and line it up as if to print an address. (Unless it's a laser printer in which case you should line up the address on ordinary paper before using special laser printer labels.)

2   TYPE the command **copy con prn**

3   When the cursor moves down to the next line, type in the name and address:

            Dr Marilyn Talbot
            UG Systems Plc
            Roehampton Lane
            London SW15 9AN

Press the (ENTER) key at the end of each line of the address. It may take a couple of attempts to discover how much space you need before each line of the address.

Immediately you PRESS (Ctrl) **Z** or (F6) and then (ENTER), the address will be printed.

Activity 10.6 Setting up a mailing list

In the previous activity you typed in an address and copied it directly to the printer. Imagine that some time later you need to address another letter to the same person. Rather than typing it in all over again, this time you will copy the address to a temporary file, then to the printer and finally to a mailing list file.

1   Make up a new address and TYPE it into the temporary file as per step 3 above:

copy con address.tmp

2   COPY the address to the printer: **copy address.tmp prn**

3   ADD the temporary address to the mailing list file: **copy mail + address.tmp mail**

4   Repeat steps 1 and 3 several times, making up a new address each time you do step 1.

5   When you have finished, display the mail file by TYPING **copy mail con**

This data file can be used by the mail-merge function of a word processing package such as Word for Windows.

Hints about adding files

You have to be careful when adding files together and returning the result to the source file. If you get the files in the wrong order you will see the rather frightening error message:

```
Contents of destination lost before copy
```

The syntax of the file addition feature of the **copy** command you just used is:

```
copy source + [file] [+ ...] source
```

The three dots inside the second pair of brackets are called an *ellipsis.* They indicate that you can repeat the previous parameter as many times as you like, e.g.:

```
copy mail + address1 + address2  mail
```

Here the source file **mail** eventually becomes its own destination after adding one or more files to it.

When adding files together to update a master file, the safest procedure is:

1   Make a copy of the masterfile and give it the extension **.old**, e.g:

```
copy mail mail.old
```

2   Add the files together making mail the new destination file:

```
copy mail.old + address1 + address2 mail
```

The earlier version of the file before the update is now saved as **mail.old**, and the current version is called **mail**.

Activity 10.7 Another way of adding lines to a text file

Copy con is often used when you want to add a few lines to an existing file such as the **autoexec.bat** file.

Make sure there is a copy of this file in the root directory of your practice disk in **drive A**. Do not work on the real autoexec file in the root directory of your hard disk **C:**

1   To set up the activity, first TYPE the commands:

    a:
    cd
    copy c:\autoexec.bat a:\autoexec.old

2   To add some lines to the file, TYPE the command:

    copy autoexec.old + con autoexec.bat

    The computer responds:

    ```
AUTOEXEC.OLD
CON
```

3   Now you TYPE:

    rem This is an example line which won't actually do anything (ENTER)
    rem because the remark lines beginning with 'rem' are not executed. (ENTER)
    (F6) (ENTER)

4   To view your handiwork, TYPE:

    type autoexec.bat

You should see the new lines tacked on at the end. Also, you still have the old version saved as **autoexec.old** for added security. Notice that DOS sees the keyboard (**con**) as just another file which is added to the first file in the list of parameters.

The full syntax of the copy command

copy [/a |/b] source [/a |/b] [+ source[/a |/b] [+...] [destination [/a |/b] [/v]
1   2   3   4   5   6   7

1 The first word specifies the actual command.

2 [/a |/b] indicates a choice between two alternative switches /a or /b
   They are used by programmers to copy either ASCII or binary files.

3 **source** is the mandatory combination of drive, path and/or filename
   that specifies the location of the files to be copied.

4 [+ **source**] means that optional additional source files may be added.

5 [+ ...] the *ellipsis* indicates that the previous parameter may be
   repeated.

6 [**destination**] this optional parameter specifies the combination of
   destination drive, path or file. If no destination is specified, the source
   files are copied to the current, or default directory.

7 [/v] the **verify** switch confirms or verifies that the file(s) have been
   written.

Filespec

Sometimes you will see the abbreviation **filespec**, which means any
combination of drive letters, paths and filenames that make a full file
specification.

Here are some examples:

c:\dos\defrag.exe

a:*.doc

\accounts\sales???.dat

Deleting files

● To identify and delete files safely
● To recover files deleted by accident

At times you will need to remove unwanted files from a disk that has become cluttered. Users often fail to do this because they are frightened of the **delete** command in case they make a mistake and delete files that they need to keep. Failure to remove redundant files is just as bad in the long run, as disks become full, sometimes causing serious problems.

In Activity 9.3 you should have copied a number of files into the subdirectory A:\PRACTICE. You will learn how to purge the directory using the **del** (delete) command confidently. It is important to be certain that the file specification [**filespec**] parameter is correct, so you will be shown how to check the **filespec** before performing the actual deletion. Additional protection is given by the **undelete** command (see page 49).

There are four steps involved in the safe deletion of files:

1   Use **dir [filespec]** to check the location of the files to be deleted.

2   Move to the directory where the files are located.

3   Use **del** with the same **filespec** as you did with **dir**.

This way you can be certain that the files to be deleted are the same ones you just listed and checked.

4   Finally, use **dir** to check that the correct files have been deleted.

If you suspect that a mistake has been made and that a file or files have been deleted in error, it is possible to recover them provided action is taken promptly (see page 49).

Warning

Be very careful to do these activities using your practice disk. Check that the root directory of **drive A** is the current directory.

Do not continue with these activities if the system prompt indicates that the current directory is located on drive C.

If you are working at a diskless network station, consult the network manager before attempting these activities.

Command syntax

del [filespec] [/p]

Don't forget that **[filespec]** can be any combination of drive, path and file specification including the **?** and ***** wildcards.

e.g. `del a:\word\memo.doc /p`

In practice the **confirmation prompt /p** switch is rarely used. The combination of **dir** and **del** provides enough protection against accidental erasure.

The word **erase** may be substituted for **del** if preferred; thus the command **erase letter3.doc** is perfectly valid.

Activity 11.1 Deleting a single file

On page 34 you were shown how to make some files beginning with the letters **ex** by redirecting the output of **dir**. Now is the time to delete them. You could do this in one single operation using the filespec **ex*.*** but this would delete all other files beginning with **ex** and we'll assume that you may wish to keep some of them. To start with you can practise by deleting one file at a time.

1   Use **dir** to locate and identify the file to be deleted.

   TYPE **dir ex1.lst /s**

   Take care to differentiate between **1** and **l**, the small **L**.

2   Change to the directory where the files are located.

   TYPE **cd \practice**

3   Use the same filespec as you did in step 1, but omit **/s**. You might like to use the **/p** switch which prompts you to confirm deletion of the specified file.

   TYPE **del ex1.lst /p**

4   Type **dir** again to see that **ex1.lst** should no longer be listed.

Repeat steps 2 and 3 to identify and delete the file **ex2.lst**. Finally, check using **dir** that the correct file has been deleted.

Activity 11.2 Deleting a group of files using the wildcards

Suppose you want to delete all the remaining files that begin with the **ex** combination. You could do this by typing **del ex*.***, but be careful, as there may be other files beginning with the letters **ex** that you want to keep. Follow the four-step rule:

1   Specify and locate the exact set of files you want to delete by TYPING **dir ex*.* /s**

Your computer will respond something like this:

```
Directory of A:\PRACTICE

ex1.dir
ex2.dir
ex10.txt

3 File(s) 3041 bytes
```

2   Change to the correct subdirectory by TYPING **cd \practice**

At this point you may decide that you wish to delete only those files with extension **dir**. You can safely use the filespec **ex*.dir** to delete both files at once.

3   TYPE **del ex*.dir**

4   TYPE **dir** again to see which files remain in the directory.

See if there are any other groups of files that were copied to the root directory of the **A drive**. They can probably be specified using the * wildcard, together with extensions like **.exe .com .sys** and **.bat**. Then follow the four steps and continue to delete until no files are left. Notice that the subdirectories are not erased by **del**.

Activity 11.3 Deleting the entire contents of a directory in one operation

If you know the directory where files are located you can reverse the order of steps one and two of the four-step rule.

1   Change to the directory where files to be deleted are located: **cd \practice\accounts**

2   Use **dir** to check exactly which files are there: **dir /p**

3   If you are certain that the entire list should be deleted, TYPE **del *.***

When you use ***.*** as the parameter, you will see the message: `Are you sure, (Y/N)?`

4   PRESS **Y** or **N** (ENTER) as appropriate.

Taking precautions against accidental erasure

When you see the message **Are you sure, Y/N?** it gives you a chance to change your mind; if you are in any doubt at all, press **N** and type **dir** once more so that you can have another careful look at the directory listing. Only if you are quite certain should you press **Y** (ENTER) which gives permission to delete all the files in that directory.

It is possible to protect all the files on a disk from accidental erasure by having the write-protect slot covered. Remove the practice disk from **drive A** and take a closer look at it. At the bottom left of the 3.5 inch plastic disks there is a little black switch at the back that can be moved so that you can no longer see any light through the square hole.

On the old style 5.25 inch floppies there is a **write-protect notch** near the top right of the diskette as you look at the label. To protect the disk the notch has to be covered with a **write-protect tab** which is nothing more than a piece of sticky metallic tape.

These methods are similar to the way in which audio and video cassettes can be protected by removing the plastic lugs at the back of the cartridge. Whilst protecting the files on the disk from accidental erasure it also prevents you from editing or updating the files.

Activity 11.4 Investigating a protected disk

Protect your practice disk by setting it to **read-only**. Do this by moving the switch or by covering the notch with metallic tape depending on the type of disk.

1   Make sure that **drive A** is the current drive, by TYPING **a:**

2   Look for a subdirectory where there are still some files, TYPE: **dir /s**

3   TYPE **cd** followed by the directory name.

4   Try deleting all the files there by TYPING **del *.***

If you have correctly set the disk to read-only, DOS will return the message: `Access denied`

5   Now try to copy files to the disk. TYPE **copy c:**

Notice that you can **read** from the disk (this has been proved by the fact **dir** still works) but you can't **write** to the disk, thereby effectively disabling commands like **copy** and **del**.

6   Finally, remove the physical write-protection from your practice disk by resetting the switch or peeling off the tab.

Undeleting files

You used not to be able to undelete files in earlier versions of DOS unless you had a special utility program purchased separately from DOS. When you delete a file using the **del** command, DOS removes the filename from the disk directory and releases the space it occupied for other files that may be written to the disk at a later time. Provided that no new file is written to the disk immediately after a file has been deleted, it should be possible to recover the deleted file by using the **undelete** command.

Activity 11.5 Using the undelete command

1 Make sure that **drive A** is the current drive, by TYPING **a:**

2 Look for a subdirectory where there are still some files: **dir /s**

3 Make that the current directory by TYPING **cd** followed by the directory name.

4 Delete a group of files, e.g. **del *.lst**

5 TYPE the command **undelete**

The response from your computer will look something like this:

```
A:\PRACTICE>undelete

Directory: A:\PRACTICE
File specifications: *.*

    Deletion tracking file not found.

    MS-DOS directory contains 1 deleted files
    Of those, 1 files may be recovered.

Using the MS-DOS directory.

        ?utoexecbat    356  01-01-92  3:19  Undelete (Y/N) ?y
        Please type the first character for ?utoexec.bak: a

File successfully undeleted.
```

Unless you are prepared to install the more advanced features of **undelete**, you will have to try to remember the first character of the file you want to recover, as in the example above, **?utoexec.bat**.

If you know the name of the file to be recovered you can include it as the parameter, e.g. **undelete autoexec.bat**

Don't panic!

If you delete an important file by mistake, you should:

1 Recover it from the backup copy that you always meant to make, but on this occasion no doubt you forgot!

2 Use the **undelete** command, or a third party utility such as Norton Utilities if you have one.

3 If **undelete** fails to work, remove the disk from the drive if the lost file was a on a floppy disk. If the file was on the hard disk, switch off the computer and, if necessary, disable it by removing the power cable or disconnecting the keyboard. These measures are to prevent another user from inadvertantly creating a new file in the space released by the deleted one. You should then use a disk doctor utility package to try to recover the file.

4 When the computer is up and running again, back up important files before you do anything else!!

How to avoid trouble

The best ways to avoid losing files by careless deletion are:

1 Always change to the drive and directory where the file(s) are located before attempting to delete them.

2 Always use **dir** to check the **filespec** parameter you intend to use with **del**. If the filespec identifies the correct files with **dir**, the same **filespec** will work with **del**.

MS-DOS 6 undelete upgrade

The **undelete** command has been further upgraded in MS-DOS 6. Two higher levels of protection are offered by making part of the **undelete** program memory resident. The highest protection is called **Delete Sentry**, invoked by placing the command **undelete /s** in the autoexec.bat file or by typing the command at the system prompt. The medium level is called **Delete Tracker**, which is enabled by the **/t** switch. The lowest, or default level is virtually the same as the version 5 **undelete** command described above.

There is also a new WINDOWS version of the program. Detailed information is given in MS-DOS 6 **help**, and in the MS-DOS 6 Upgrade Manual.

If you follow the advice given earlier on this page, you should be able to use the default setting to recover from an accidental deletion provided that you do it without delay.

Removing subdirectories

- To locate and remove subdirectories
- To delete a branch of the tree (MS-DOS 6 only)

Occasionally a subdirectory will become redundant and you will want to remove it in order to tidy up the disk. The remove directory command is **rmdir**, but normally we use the abbreviated form **rd**.

Command syntax

rd [drive:]path

e.g.

```
rd a:\practice
```

To remove a directory it must be empty of files and it cannot be the current directory. The most secure place to be when removing a directory is the parent directory.

Make sure that your practice disk is in **drive A** and make **\practice** the current directory. Look at the diagram of your practice disk's directory structure on page 24 before starting the following activity.

Activity 12.1 Removing the accounts subdirectory

1 Try to remove the subdirectory **accounts** by TYPING **rd accounts**

   You will see the error message:

   ```
   Invalid path, not directory or directory not empty
   ```

   This is because the **accounts** directory still has files in it.

2 Follow the four-step rule and delete the files in the **accounts** directory:

   cd accounts
   dir *.*
   del *.*
   dir

3 Drop back to the parent directory by TYPING:

   cd ..

---

4   Now TYPE **rd accounts**

The same error message will be displayed. Although the **accounts** directory is now empty of files, you will have seen from the last **dir** listing that the **sales, purchase** and **nominal** subdirectories are still attached. Any files they contain will have to be deleted, then the subdirectories must themselves be removed before **accounts** can be removed.

Activity 12.2 Removing the child directories

1   Change to the **sales** directory by TYPING **cd sales**

2   Delete the files there by TYPING the commands:

   dir *.*
   del *.*
   dir

3   Drop back to the parent directory and remove the child, by TYPING:

   cd . .   (. . is the code for parent)
   rd sales

4   Try to remove the directories **purchase** and **nominal**:

   rd purchase
   rd nominal

If you get the usual error message, the directories will have to be cleared of files before you can proceed to remove them. In that case, you will have to repeat steps 1, 2 and 3 again, substituting the names **nominal** and **purchase** in place of sales.

Activity 12.3 Removing the wpro branch of the tree

To do this you will have to drop back another level to the **\practice** directory which is the parent of **wpro**. However, by now you will have realised that there is little point in doing this unless you have first cleared all the files out of the child directories belonging to that branch.

If you have done the previous activities you should be able to work out the actual commands for yourself. Follow the steps:

1 Change to the outermost subdirectory to be removed.

2 Use **dir** to check that the files there are OK to delete.

3 If, so delete all of them.

4 Drop back one level.

5 Remove the empty child directory.

Repeat the procedure until all the **wpro** subdirectories have been removed.

Activity 12.4 Using the new MS-DOS 6 command 'deltree'

Deltree deletes a directory and all the files and subdirectories below it in one fell stroke!

Make sure that the current drive is **drive A**. To delete a subdirectory branch you must be in the parent directory.

1 TYPE the commands:

a:
**cd **
deltree practice

If you have MS-DOS installed, the computer will respond:

```
Delete directory "practice" and all its subdirectories [yn] y
Deleting practice...
```

Deltree certainly makes tidying up disks a whole lot easier. It is formidably powerful and you should exercise the same care you learned when deleting files. There is a **/y** switch which disables the yes/no prompt. This is for use in DOS batch programs; it would be extreme folly for interactive users to disable the **yn** prompt.

Renaming files and directories

● To rename files using the **copy** and **rename** commands
● To rename a directory using the MS-DOS 6 command **move**

When you used the **copy** command in Tasks 9 and 10, you were copying files from one device or directory to another by creating duplicate files on the destination device. It is also possible, using **copy**, to create a duplicate file with a different name from that of the source file. This is extremely useful where you wish to create a standard document or template which will require different versions from time to time.

Revision

Setting up a practice directory for Task 13.

1 Make sure that you are in the root directory of **drive A**.

2 Make a directory called TASK13

3 Change to that directory.

4 Copy into the new directory the system .sys files from C:\ or wherever they are located on your hard disk.

If you can't remember how to do this, the commands are listed on the next page.

Activity 13.1 Making duplicate files with different names

You should be in the TASK13 directory and the system prompt should show: A:\TASK13>

1 TYPE **dir config.sys** to check that there is now a file in **A:** called **config.sys**

2 Make two copies of the file called **config1.sys** and **config2.sys** by TYPING:

copy config.sys config1.sys

copy config.sys config2.sys

If you had problems setting up the practice directory, TYPE the following
commands:

a:
**cd **
md task13
cd task13
copy c:*.sys

Activity 13.2 Copying a group of files and changing the names

This time you can copy all the **.sys** files in **C:** to your **\task13** directory, but the new files
should all have the suffix **.sy$**

1 TYPE **copy c:*.sys   a:*.sy$**
      dir *.sy?

Do the same thing with all the **.bat** files, but change the names of the duplicates to **.bak**

2 TYPE **copy c:*.bat a:*.bak**
      dir *.ba?

Activity 13.3 Renaming a single file using ren

If you want to rename a file without creating a duplicate copy, you should use the **rename**, or
ren command.

1 To rename the file **config.sys** to **config.old**, TYPE **ren config.sys config.old**

2 Then check what has happened by TYPING **dir conf***

3 TYPE **ren config1.sys config.sys**

4 TYPE **dir conf***

What happens if you try to rename **config2.sys** to **config.sys**?

5 TYPE **ren config2.sys config.sys**

   Because the file **config.sys** already exists in the same directory, you will see the error
   message:

   ```
   Duplicate file name or file not found
   ```

Command syntax for rename

rename [drive:][path] filename1 filename2

e.g. `rename a:\text\memo.asc memo.txt`

It is rather less confusing to change to the drive and directory where the file to be renamed is located and to use the **rename** command there. In the example above, the renamed file **memo.txt** remains on **drive A** in the directory **\text**.

Activity 13.4 Renaming a directory in MS-DOS 6 using 'move'

If you have MS-DOS 6 installed, you can use the new **move** command to rename a directory.

To rename the directory **a:\task13** to **a:\activity**, you should change to the parent directory:

1   TYPE **a:**
      **cd **

2   TYPE **move task13 activity**

3   To see your changes, list the directories by TYPING **dir /ad**

Renaming a directory in MS-DOS 5

Before MS-DOS 6, the only way to rename a directory was this rather long-winded series of steps:

1   Create the new directory.

2   Copy files from the old directory.

3   Use **dir** to check that they are all present.

4   Delete the original files.

5   Remove the old directory.

Tidying up

When you have finished Task 13 you should delete the practice files in **a:\task13** and then remove the directory. If you have MS-DOS 6 installed you will be able to do this in one single operation using the new **deltree** command.

Section D
Disks and security

| Task 14 | Formatting a floppy disk

- To format a floppy disk
- To create a boot disk
- To minimise the risks of destroying data

New floppy disks are usually supplied unformatted, in boxes of ten. Before they can be used in the computer to store programs or data they have to be formatted. This process creates an invisible pattern of magnetic tracks on the disk together with an empty directory and a table called the File Allocation Table (FAT) which allocates disk space to each file as it is created and updated. When a file is deleted the free space is returned to the FAT. Previously formatted disks can be formatted again, but **all data will be lost.** It is therefore most important to take care when using this command.

MS-DOS will not recognise a floppy disk which is either unformatted or has been formatted by another operating system. For instance, disks from Apple microcomputers, BBC micros and Ataris cannot normally be used in an IBM-compatible PC running MS-DOS.

Units of storage

Even within the DOS family, there are various formats which depend on disk size and density. The more tracks there are on the disk, the more data can be stored on it. The size or extent of a file is measured in bytes. One byte can store the equivalent of one alphanumeric character. The larger units of storage are Kilobytes, Megabytes and Gigabytes. 1 Kilobyte, abbreviated to 1K, is equal to 1024 bytes. 1 Megabyte, abbreviated to 1Mb is equal to 1024K, which is just over a million bytes. A Gigabyte is the same as 1024Mb.

Disk types

MS-DOS recognises eight different disk types of which four are in common use:

5.25 inch double-sided/double density	360K
5.25 inch double-sided/quad density	1.2Mb
3.5 inch double-sided/double density	720K
3.5 inch double-sided/high density	1.44Mb

In order to format disks to quad or high density specification, the disks themselves must be designated for the purpose. The quality of the magnetic coating has to be finer; otherwise, even if you are successful in achieving the higher format, the disk will be unreliable and data will be lost or corrupted, leading to unpredictable results.

Since disks are used to carry and exchange data between PCs that are not connected by a network, it is useful to know how to prepare disks to the four most common formats. Older computers may have disk-drive units that can read data only from double density disks; even if your computer can read/write all formats, you may need to be able to produce disks at the lower specification so that a friend or colleague can share data with you. Disk sharing is one of the most common ways of transmitting computer viruses, so read Task 20 before exchanging disks with other users.

Preparing for the activities

You will need some floppy disks to try out the activities that follow. What you do from now on will depend on the configuration of your computer. Providing you follow the instructions carefully you will do no harm even if you try formatting a disk to the wrong density. The only truly silly thing to do would be to reformat your hard disk. This is quite a difficult task given the warning messages that appear. None of the commands suggested to you in the Activities will endanger the data on your hard disk.

Try to get hold of both a double density and a high or quad density disk. The disks need not be brand new, but don't forget, if they are old disks, all data or programs will be wiped out by the formatting process.

Activity 14.1 Formatting a practice disk

Make sure you have a new disk available to put into the appropriate drive. The instructions in the Training Guide will normally assume the disk to be formatted is in **drive A**. However, if you have two floppy disk drives, and **drive A** takes 5.25 inch disks and **drive B** takes 3.5 inch disks, you can substitute **drive B** for **drive A** if you have put a 3.5in disk into the drive.

Unless you specify otherwise, the basic command will format the disk to High Density standard. If your disk does not indicate **HD**, proceed with the Activity but expect different results.

1   Insert the floppy disk into the appropriate drive.

2   TYPE the command **format a:** or **format b:** as appropriate.

The MS-DOS **format** messages refer to floppy disks as **diskettes**. Various responses will be required from you: see the example below and the comments in the shaded boxes.

If you have put an HD 3.5in disk into the drive, the computer will respond like this:

```
Insert new diskette for drive A:
and press ENTER when ready...

Checking existing disk format.
Saving UNFORMAT information.
Verifying 1.44M

1 percent completed.
Format complete.

Volume label (11 characters,
ENTER for none)? practice2

1457664 bytes total disk space
1457664 bytes available on disk

512 bytes in each allocation unit.
847 allocation units available.

Volume Serial Number is 284E-1AFF

Format another (Y/N)?n
```

Even if there is already a disk in the drive, you must still PRESS the (ENTER) key.

If the disk is not new and is very full, you may get an error message at this point. See p 60.

You will see a display indicating what percentage of the disk has been formatted.

Finally, you may give the disk a name or label.

If the number of bytes available on disk is less than the total disk space, it means that your disk has some bad sectors. This is all right unless the difference is greater than about 64K.

Press N if you do not wish to format another disk.

Troubleshooting

`Bad command or filename`

Format is an external command, so you must make sure that the **path** variable has been set so that the command can be found and executed (see Task 22). Alternatively, you could use **dir \format.com /s** to find the directory where the command is located. Change to that directory and type the command again.

`Incorrect DOS version`

TYPE the command **ver**. It is possible that you have DOS external commands including **format** that belong to an earlier version of MS-DOS. Alternatively, for some reason the computer has been booted up with the earlier version and now you are trying to use a later version of **format**.

The formatting process gets slower and slower or the computer 'hangs'

Even if the process does finish, the final display will indicate far fewer bytes available than the total indicated disk space. This is most likely because the disk you are using is not a High Density disk. See Activity 14.2 below.

Activity 14.2 Formatting double density disks

You can try this activity with any type of 3.5 or 5.25 inch disk.

To format a 3.5 inch disk to 720K density you should use the **/f:size** switch. You should substitute 720 or 360 for the **size** parameter, depending on the disk capacity.

1 TYPE the command **format a: /f:720**

To format a double-density 5.25 inch disk, you set size to 360.

2 TYPE the command **format a: /f:360**

Don't forget, you **must** use the appropriate drive letter, **a:** or **b:**

If you had problems trying to format your double density disk using the default format command, this should remedy the situation.

TYPE in a suitable **volume label** when requested. It helps to identify the disk later on.

Activity 14.3 Creating a boot disk

You should always have a spare floppy disk available from which to boot the computer in case the hard disk becomes faulty. The **/s** switch transfers the system files **io.sys, msdos.sys** and **command.com** to the specified floppy disk.

1   Select and insert the size of disk that fits your **A drive**.

2   If the **A drive** uses 5.25 inch disks, TYPE **format a: /f:360 /s**

3   If the **A drive** uses 3.5 inch disks, TYPE **format a: /f:720 /s**

4   When prompted for a volume label, TYPE **boot disk**

    If the command executes successfully, the following message will be displayed:

    ```
    System transferred
    ```

5   TYPE **dir /ah** to see the three files including the hidden **.sys** files.

Activity 14.4 Rebooting the computer: the cold boot

In order to test out your new boot disk, you need to reset the computer. The contents of memory are lost when the computer is reset. In order to start up again, the low level ROM BIOS program looks for MS-DOS on **drive A** first, and if that fails, it looks on **drive C**.

1   Switch off the power, pausing for a few moments until no further disk drive activity can be heard.

2   Place your new boot disk in **drive A** and switch on the power.

You will not see any of the familar things that happen when you boot up normally since these are loaded up from files on the hard disk. The default prompt **A>** will show that the computer has booted from the floppy disk, so your usual default path will not have been set.

3   TYPE **path**

    ```
    no path
    ```

4   Take your boot disk out of **drive A**.

5   Switch the power off, then on again, so as to reboot the computer from the hard disk. Try the **path** command again. This time your usual path should be displayed.

Park the hard disk when shutting off the power!

Most PCs supplied since about 1991 usually have auto head parking facilities. If your computer is older, then you should park the disk drive heads before shutting off the power. This removes the heads from the disk surface, which is particularly important if the computer is to be moved.

If the heads are in contact with a stationary disk surface on a regular basis, there is always the risk of damage or data corruption. If there is a disk parking utility on your hard disk, it will be there because it was supplied with a disk drive that does require parking, so use it!

Typical disk parking programs are called **park, dpark, shipdisk.**

Activity 14.5 Rebooting the computer: the warm boot

You can also reset the computer without switching off the power by pressing the RESET button or using the [Ctrl] [Alt] [Del] combination. Starting up after such a procedure is called a **warm boot.**

1 Place your new boot disk in **drive A.**

2 PRESS the RESET button, if there is one, or HOLD down the [Ctrl] and [Alt] keys and then PRESS the [Del] key.

Again, the default prompt will show **A>** and your usual default path will not have been set.

3 TYPE **path**

   no path

4 Take your boot disk out of **drive A.**

5 Reboot the computer from the hard disk by following step 2.

6 TYPE **path**

If you do not already have a floppy boot disk, replace the write-protect tab or move the switch to read-only on this your new boot disk and put it away safely. It could get you out of trouble if the computer fails to boot from the hard disk or is infected with a virus.

Some useful format switches

/q

The **quick format** utility can be used to reformat an already formatted disk. The switch causes the old disk directory and File Allocation Table to be deleted. The disk is not scanned for bad sectors, so take this short cut only if you know the disk is in good condition.

/s

The **system** switch transfers operating system files so as to make a boot disk.

/u

The **unconditional** format switch speeds up formatting by omitting warning messages and preventing later unformatting. **Do not use it.**

/v:label   e.g. /v:accounts

Enables the volume label to be specified on the command line. This is useful if you want to format a number of disks which all require the same volume label.

/4 and /8

These switches specify 360K format on a 5.25 inch disk when using a 1.2Mb drive. If an older computer has difficulty reading from disks formatted on a newer machine using the size switch **/f:360**, try either of these switches instead.

Unformatting a disk

Sooner or later the time always comes when you suddenly realise that you did after all want some of the data on a disk that is now being formatted. Or perhaps a friend or colleague is howling in despair having just accidentally formatted their hard disk. You can now spring to the rescue, assuming:

1 **The computer is running MS-DOS 5 or 6.**

2 **Nothing has been saved on the disk after the accidental format.**

3 **The disk was not formatted using the /u switch. (I told you not to use it!)**

Try the experiments in the next activity to help you learn more about the way the format/unformat process works.

Activity 14.6 Unformatting a disk

1 Take one of your newly formatted disks, place it in **drive A** and TYPE **a:**

2 Copy some files from **drive C** by TYPING **copy c:**

3 TYPE **dir** and make a mental note of the files.

4 If it is a 3.5 inch disk, format it by TYPING **format a:** /f:720

5 If it is a 5.25 inch disk, TYPE **format a:** /f:360

6 After the format procedure has finished, TYPE **dir**

   File not found

So now the files on the disk have been destroyed by the formatting process. Let's see if they can be recovered by unformatting the disk.

7 TYPE **unformat a:**

8 TYPE **dir** to see if the files have all been restored.

You might like to try the procedure again, except that in place of step 6 you should copy one or two files from a different directory of **drive C**. This will inevitably cause problems.

You could also try formatting an old disk which is no longer required. Then **unformat** it and see if the files have been restored.

Duplicating a disk

- To make a duplicate copy of a floppy disk
- To compare the two disks

The external command **diskcopy** copies the contents of the floppy disk in the source drive to a formatted or unformatted disk in the target drive. In the case of a single disk drive machine, MS-DOS will keep telling you which disk to put into the drive.

Warning! All data on the target disk will be destroyed by this operation, so you should afford this command the same degree of respect as you did the **format** command. **Diskcopy** works only with floppy disks of the same type.

You will need two floppy disks of the same type for this exercise. The source disk should have some files on it, so copy some from the hard disk before you begin. You could use your new boot disk as the source disk.

Activity 15.1 **Diskcopy on a computer with one floppy drive**

1 Fix a write-protect tab to the source disk, or move the switch on a 3.5 inch disk so that you can see the light through it.

2 TYPE **a:**

3 TYPE **diskcopy**

Diskcopy will tell you when to put the appropriate disks into the drive.

Typical output from the command will look like this:

```
Insert SOURCE diskette in drive A:

Press any key to continue . . .

Copying 40 tracks
9 sectors/track, 2 Side(s)

Insert target diskette in drive A:
Press any key when ready . . .

Copy another diskette (Y/N)? n
```

If your computer has less memory than the capacity of the floppy disk to be copied, you will have to swap the two disks several times.

Troubleshooting

`Bad command or filename`

If the command did not work then it is because you still don't have the path set up properly, see Task 22.

`TARGET diskette bad or incompatible`
`Copy process ended`

This may mean quite literally what it says, that is, the target disk you have supplied has been damaged or corrupted.

Alternatively it may mean that the disk has been formatted by another type of computer altogether such as an Atari. A further reason could be that the target disk type does not match the source disk. If you look back up the display that **diskcopy** provides, you may see this message:

> `Copying 80 tracks`
> `15 sectors per track, 2 side(s)`

Although **diskcopy** is supposed to recognise a target disk with a lower capacity than the source and display the message:

> `TARGET media has lower capacity than SOURCE`
> `Continue anyway (Y/N)?`

In practice this does not always happen and you get the `bad or incompatible` error message above.

`Invalid drive specification`
`Specified drive does not exist`
`or is non-removable`

If you see the invalid drive error message it will probably be because you have failed to specify the correct disk drive for the source and/or target disks. When you are logged on to **drive C** and type the command **diskcopy** with no drive parameters you will certainly see the error message above.

Either, you should be logged into drive A, as I recommend in the Activities, in which case you can type **diskcopy** with no parameters, **or,** if you're on **drive C** you would have to type **diskcopy a:** or **diskcopy a: b:**

Activity 15.2 Diskcopy on a computer with two identical floppy drives

It's much easier to perform a **diskcopy** when you have two identical disk drives. Have two disks of the same size and capacity ready. It is always a good idea to **write-protect** the source disk, just in case you make a mistake. Stick on the metal tab or move the little plastic switch as appropriate.

1   Put the **source** disk into **drive A** and the **target** disk into **drive B**.

2   TYPE **a:**

3   TYPE **diskcopy a: b:**

If the new copy is to be a backup disk, transfer the physical write-protection from the source disk to the target disk before putting the disks away carefully. Write-protection must always be removed if the disk is to be returned to normal use.

Activity 15.3 Using the diskcomp command to compare two floppy disks

If you want to check a pair of disks because you are not certain whether they are true copies of one another, you should use the **diskcomp** command. Use the same two disks as in the previous Activity. The same rules about similar disks apply as with **diskcopy**.

1   If you have a machine with one floppy disk drive, place the first disk in the floppy drive.

2   TYPE **a:**

3   TYPE **diskcomp** and follow the instructions to change disks.

If you have a machine with two identical drives you can put one disk into each drive, log on to **drive A**, then TYPE **diskcomp a: b:**

You may like to copy a file to one of the two disks and then try the command again. Compare the output with the examples on the next page.

Output from diskcomp

If the two disks compare favourably, you will see the message:

```
Compare OK
```

If there are differences, you will see a message like this:

```
Compare error on
side 1, track 3
```

If one of the disks was made using the **copy** command as opposed to the **diskcopy** command, but the files are identical, you may see a message like:

```
Compare error on
side 0, track 0
```

If the disks and drives are not compatible with one another, you will see this error message:

```
Drive types or diskette types not compatible
```

If you remain logged on to the hard disk and do not specify the correct floppy drive parameters, you will see the same error message that **diskcopy** gives in similar circumstances:

```
Invalid drive specification
Specified drive does not exist
or is non-removable
```

Protecting files

- To protect files from accidental or deliberate erasure
- To investigate and change file attributes

Each file can have up to four **attributes** associated with it:

The **read-only** attribute determines whether you may update or delete the file.

The **archive** attribute determines whether the file is selected for backing up by the **backup** or **xcopy** commands.

The **hidden and system file** attributes prevent the file from being listed by **dir.**

Each attribute is indicated by a flag corresponding to its initial letter.

Activity 16.1 Setting a file to read-only

You will create a new file on your practice disk, check its file attributes, set it to **read-only**, then see what happens when you try to update or delete it.

1 Put your practice disk in **drive A** and log on to that drive by TYPING **a:**

2 TYPE **echo To test the attrib command >special.doc**

3 TYPE the command **type special.doc**

4 TYPE **attrib special.doc**

    A   A:\SPECIAL.DOC

5 TYPE **echo which can protect your files >>special.doc**

6 TYPE **attrib +r special.doc**

7 TYPE **echo try updating the file now >>special.doc**

Notes on steps 2 to 6

2 You created the file by redirecting the output from **echo** to the file using the redirect > symbol.

3 Use the **type** command to display the file contents.

4 The **attrib** flag **A** shows that the default status is Archive only.

5 You may type another **echo** statement to update the file using the redirect and update >> symbols.

6 You protect the file by adding the read-only parameter +r to the command. Step 7 should now fail and you will see the **Access denied** error message.

Activity 16.2 Using wild characters with attrib

1 Display the current attributes of all files in the working directory by TYPING **attrib**

2 You can protect all the files in a directory with the command **attrib +r a:*.***

3 Now try deleting all the files by typing **del a:*.***

```
Access denied
```

In reality you should be rather more selective about which files to protect in a given directory. It would be very sensible to move to a directory containing both programs and data files and to protect the programs only by TYPING commands like:

attrib +r *.exe

attrib +r *.com

attrib +r .ovl

Activity 16.3 Changing the archive flag

The **xcopy** and **backup** commands (see Tasks 17 and 18) inspect the archive attribute, or flag to determine whether the file should be included in a general backup operation.

You have already seen that a newly created file has its archive flag set by default. Look again at the attributes of the file **special.doc**

1 TYPE **attrib special.doc**

```
A    H         A:\SPECIAL.DOC
```

2 TYPE **attrib -a -r special.doc**

3 Inspect the result by TYPING **attrib special.doc**

4 TYPE **echo updating the file once more >>special.doc**

5 TYPE **attrib special.doc**

```
A    A:\SPECIAL.DOC
```

Notes on the steps

1 You should see that both archive and read-only flags are set.

2 Uses the minus sign to remove an attribute.

3 The attribute flags A H should no longer show up in the output.

4 Uses the echo and redirect technique to update the file once more.

5 You should see that the archive flag has been reset, indicating that the file has indeed been updated and will require backing up once more.

File security

Occasionally you may need to keep particularly sensitive material in a file on the hard disk of a machine that is shared with other users. Of course you could work with the file on a separate floppy disk which you remove after use. However, there are times when this is not convenient, so one remedy is to make the file into a **hidden file**. Unless the level of DOS knowledge of your colleagues (and their nosiness and determination) is high, the protection afforded by hiding the file when you are not using it is usually sufficient to deter purely opportunist snooping.

Similar protection may be achieved using the **system file** attribute.

Activity 16.4 Investigating the hidden file attribute

Select a file on your practice disk that you would like to hide, e.g. **special.doc**

1   Make sure that the file is not set to read-only, so TYPE **attrib -r special.doc**

2   Set the file to hidden status by TYPING **attrib +h special.doc**

3   TYPE **dir spec*.***

4   You should be able to list the file by TYPING **dir /ah**
    (**/ah** is the **dir** 'attribute hidden' switch).

5   Try to delete the file by TYPING **del special.doc**

    ```
    File not found
    ```

Hiding the file protects it from accidental deletion; **delete** simply doesn't know it's there! Can the file be updated? Try the next step:

6   TYPE **echo attempting to add a line to hidden file >>special.doc**

7   TYPE **type special.doc**

You should be able to see the extra line, proving that hiding a file does not make it truly read-only. Whether or not a hidden file can be loaded into a word processor will probably vary from package to package.

Activity 16.5 Setting the system file flag

System files consist of programs, device drivers and data files that determine the configuration and functioning of the computer. Files which have the system attribute flag set will not be listed by **dir** unless the **/as** switch is used.

1   Log on to the root directory of **drive C**.

2   Locate files ending with **.sys** by TYPING **dir *.sys /s**

3   If the **.sys** files are not in the root directory, change to the directory you have located.

4   Copy the **.sys** files from **drive C** by TYPING **copy *.sys a:**

5   Log on to your practice disk in **drive A**.

6   Set the system and read-only flags by TYPING **attrib +s +r *.sys**

7   TYPE **dir *.sys**

8   TYPE **dir /as**

9   TYPE **attrib *.sys**

Command syntax

The general form of the command is:

attrib [+ | -r] [+ | -a] [+ | -s] [+ | -h] [drive: path filename] [/s]

Notice that all the parameters are optional, as indicated by the square brackets.

If no parameters are specified, **attrib** will display the flag settings of the attributes belonging to the files in the default directory.

The flags are set or removed by the plus or minus sign before the initial letter of the flag.

Appropriate combinations of drive letters, paths and filenames can be substituted for the parameters in italics.

The **/s** switch processes subdirectories below the current directory.

e.g. `attrib +r +s b:\dos\*.sys /s`

Backing up directories

● To learn other ways of making secure backups of both files and directories
● To be able to decide on the most appropriate method to use

You have already learned two commands that can be used to back up data; the internal **copy** command and the external command **diskcopy**.

Copy can be used to make perfectly satisfactory backups of individual files or groups of files using the wild characters, providing that the files have a common pattern of characters in their names.

If you need to copy from various subdirectories a whole range of files whose only common property is, for instance, that they have all been created or updated since the same time last week, you would have to change directories, identify the right files and type the **copy** command several times in each directory to do it.

From MS-DOS 3.3 onwards there is a more sophisticated copy command called **xcopy**, i.e. external copy command.

The additional features of **xcopy** enable you to copy:

Directory branches together with their files

Files with the archive attribute set

Files created or updated on or after a certain date

Directory structures between disks of different formats (unlike **diskcopy**)

Setting up the activity

You will need to set up a practice directory structure on your hard disk as shown below. If you have forgotten how to do all this, you could usefully revise Task 4 which covered creating a directory structure, or look at the next page.

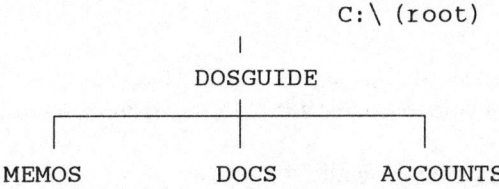

```
                         C:\ (root)
                             |
                         DOSGUIDE
          _____|_____
         |                   |                   |
      MEMOS               DOCS              ACCOUNTS
```

Copy a few small files, with endings like **.sys** and **.bat** to the first two directories.

To create and populate the practice tree

TYPE the following commands:

```
c:
cd\

md  dosguide
cd  dosguide
copy \*.bat
copy \*.sys

md  memo
md  docs
md  accounts

cd  memo
copy . .

cd . .\docs
copy . .
```

Activity 17.1 Copying an entire directory structure

Log on to **drive C** and change to your new **dosguide** directory:

1 TYPE **c:**

2 TYPE **cd dosguide**

Now copy all the .bat files from the three subdirectories to your practice disk in **drive A**:

3 TYPE **xcopy *.bat a:\ /s /e**

The **/s** switch copies subdirectories. The **/e** switch copies empty subdirectories like **accounts**.

Use the **tree** command to inspect the practice disk:

4 TYPE **tree a:\ /f**

You should see a replica of your new tree structure on **drive A** including the **.bat** files.

5 Do step 3 again, but this time copy all the **.sys** files.

Leave the floppy disk in **drive A** ready for Activity 17.2.

Activity 17.2 Copying files using the archive switches

Now you will be able to make use of the archive attribute flag that you met in Task 16.

There are two **xcopy** switches that involve this flag:

/a only those files whose archive flag is set are **xcopied**.

/m after copying the file(s) whose archive flag is set, **xcopy** clears the archive flag.

1   You should be logged on to the practice disk which is still in **drive A**.

2   TYPE **cd dosguide**

3   Delete the files there by TYPING **del *.***

4   TYPE **cd docs**

5   To inspect the file attributes TYPE **attrib**

6   Remove the archive flags from all the **.bat** files by TYPING **attrib -a *.bat**

Now you can use **xcopy** with the **/a** switch to copy files to the empty **dosguide** directory:

7   TYPE **xcopy *.* \dosguide /a**

8   TYPE **dir \dosguide**

Only the **.sys** files should have been copied, because you removed the archive flag from all the **.bat** files in step 6.

Activity 17.3 Using the /m switch

Try to work out the commands yourself. Answers are on the next page if you're really stuck!

1   Remove the archive flags from the **.sys** files in the **docs** directory.

2   Replace the archive flags you removed from the **.bat** files.

3   Use **xcopy** with the **/m** switch to copy only the files with archive flags to **\dosguide**.

4   Inspect the source files to see the status of the archive flags after this operation.

If you were succesful the **.bat** files should have been copied and their archive flags should have been removed. By using **xcopy /m** regularly, you can selectively back up only those files that have changed since the last backup.

Answers to Activity 17.3

The current directory should be **a:\dosguide\docs**, then TYPE:

attrib -a *.bat

attrib +a *.sys

xcopy *.* \dosguide /m

attrib

Activity 17.4 Using xcopy with the date switch

You will check the date, then create a couple of new files which will be stamped with today's date so that you can test the **xcopy** date switch.

You should still be in the directory **a:\dosguide\docs**

1 TYPE **date**

2 PRESS (ENTER) if the date displayed is correct, or TYPE in today's date as shown.

3 To create a test file, TYPE **echo Activity 17.4 >test1**

4 Create another by redirecting the output from **dir** by TYPING **dir >test2**

5 Now copy only those files created today into the accounts directory by TYPING:

xcopy *.* . .\accounts /d:date

You must substitute the correct **date** into the final parameter. For instance if you wanted to copy all the files in various directories that had been amended on or after 1 October 1993, you would type the command:

xcopy *.* a:\ /d:01-10-93 /s

6 TYPE **dir \dosguide\accounts** to check that the two test files have been correctly copied.

Summary of xcopy

The general syntax of the command looks like this:

xcopy source [destination] [/a|/m][/d:date][/s [/e]][/p][/v][/w]

source You must specify the location and names of the files to be copied. If you omit the drive and path, then files will be copied from the current directory.

destination You can specify the optional destination as a **filespec** combination of drive, path and/or filename. If no destination is specified **xcopy** copies the source files to the current directory. If the source files are also in the current directory and a different destination is not specified, you will see the following error message:

```
Cannot perform a cyclic copy
```

Optional switches

/a copies only files whose archive flag is set. The flag remains set after copying.
/m copies only files whose archive flag is set. The flag is removed after copying. The destination files created by **xcopy** have their archive attribute flags set independently of the status of the source file attributes.

/d:date copies only those files updated on or after the specified date.

/s copies subdirectories below the current directory, unless they are empty.
/e copies empty subdirectories; this switch must be preceded by the **/s** switch.

/p prompts for your confirmation of each file to copy.
/v verifies each file to make sure the copy is identical to the source file(s).
/w displays a message and waits for you to press a key before starting the copy.

Restriction on xcopy

If the directory structure you are copying contains files whose capacity exceeds the target disk, you will see the disk full error message:

```
Insufficient disk space
26 file(s) copied
```

When this happens it can be quite difficult to work out how to identify the remaining files to be copied. In this case you need to use the **backup** command which is the subject of Task 18.

Making a series of backup disks

- To learn how to use the external backup commands
- To recognise the need for a series of backup disks

Although it is sensible to use **copy** and **xcopy** to back up important files and even whole subdirectories, there will be times when the space on the target disk may be too small for the files to be backed up. In such cases it is more appropriate to use the **backup** command.

With MS-DOS 6 comes the release of **Microsoft Backup**, which is Symantec's complete backup and restore utility program supplied under the Microsoft banner. The advantage of **Microsoft Backup** is that the files are also compressed, so that the number of disks required to make the backup is reduced. Files are restored from back up disks using the same program. In previous versions, files had to be restored using backup's companion program **restore**.

The MS-DOS 5 **backup** is still shipped with MS-DOS 6 so that you can restore old backups and create new ones that can be restored to computers with earlier DOS versions installed. Really old versions of **restore** (MS-DOS 3.2 or earlier) cannot be used for files backed up with versions of MS-DOS later than 3.3. But files backed up by **any** earlier version of MS-DOS can be restored using MS-DOS 5 **restore**.

Task 18 deals mainly with the MS-DOS 5 version of **backup** and its companion program **restore**. The clear documentation and ease of use of the new **Microsoft Backup** utility are so much more user-friendly that only a brief introduction will be required to get you started.

For reasons of security, the hard disk, or parts of it, should be regularly backed up to some other **media** (the name given to magnetic or other materials used for the off-line storage of data). Now that hard disks are so large, a complete backup of the MS-DOS file store to floppy disks is becoming increasingly impractical because of the large number of disks involved. Even with disk compression, the risk of muddling up the backup disks as well as the sheer amount of time it takes, means that people tend to avoid this tedious procedure, but at their peril. Backups of very high capacity hard disks are better done using 'large format' external peripheral devices such as tape streamers and cartridges. The software for making such a backup is supplied with the device.

If there is no large format off-line storage device available, sections of the hard disk will have to be backed up to a smaller, more manageable number of floppy disks. This is one very good reason for ensuring that your hard disk is sensibly arranged into a well organised tree structure.

The backup command creates one special file which stores all the source files to be backed up. The file will extend over as many floppy disks as are needed to complete the task. When the source files extend beyond the capacity of the target disk, you will be asked to load another and so on until the job is done.

Warning!

Backup erases data on the destination disk. A message will be displayed telling you that this is about to happen.

You cannot load or copy files from a backup disk using other commands like **xcopy**.

Preparing for a backup

It is important to be well organised when performing the backup operation, so have ready the following items:

Several previously formatted floppy disks, all of which must be of the same type. If the disks have not been formatted, it is possible to use the **backup** command with the **/f** switch.

If your disks are 5.25 inch type, do have enough write-protect tabs available. These are very important as you will discover.

Floppy disk labels. Unlabelled disks are a waste of time.

A marker pen; do **not** use ball point pens, especially not on 5.35 inch disks. It is better to write on the label before you stick it on to the disk.

Before you attempt Activity 18.1, look first at the sample output of steps 3 to 5 which is shown on the next page.

Activity 18.1 Backing up a small section of your hard disk

For your first attempt, try backing up the practice structure you made in Task 17.

1   Put one of your formatted practice disks into **drive A**.

2   Log on to **drive C** and change to the **dosguide** directory by TYPING:

c:
cd \dosguide

3   TYPE **backup c: a: /s**   (the **/s** switch backs up subdirectories below the current directory)

4   TYPE **dir a:**

5   TYPE **attrib a:**

```
C:\DOSGUIDE>backup c: a: /s

Insert backup diskette 01 in drive A:

WARNING! Files in the target drive
a:\root directory will be erased

Press any key to continue


*** Backing up files to drive A:***
Diskette number: 01

\DOSGUIDE\CONFIG.SYS
\DOSGUIDE\HIMEM.SYS
\DOSGUIDE\DOCS\CONFIG.SYS
\DOSGUIDE\DOCS\HIMEM.SYS
\DOSGUIDE\MEMO\AUTOEXEC.BAT
\DOSGUIDE\MEMO\WIN.BAT

C:\DOSGUIDE>dir a:

 Volume in drive A is BACKUP  001
 Volume serial number is 284E-1AFF
 Directory of A:\

BACKUP   001 34683 15-04-93 9.29p
CONTROL 001    553 15-04-93 9.29p

c:\DOSGUIDE>attrib

A    R        A:\BACKUP.001
A    R        A:\CONTROL.001
```

Notes

DOS refers to floppy disks as **diskettes.**

Although the warning is given about the root directory being erased, there is no Y/N option to proceed with the command. If at this stage you wish to abort the process, HOLD down the ⎡Ctrl⎤ key and PRESS **C**

The diskette sequence number is given. This is extremely useful when a large format backup is underway. The files and directories are listed as they are backed up.

The **dir** listing shows that a sequenced volume label is automatically written.

Because we used the backup command's **/s** switch, subdirectories have been backed up. All the files and directories have ended up together in one backup file called BACKUP.001 This is perfectly correct.

Attrib shows that the special backup files have their read-only attribute flags set automatically.

Keep the backup disk as you will need it in Task 19 to learn how to use the **restore** command.

Activity 18.2 Preparing to back up to a series of disks

If you want to try this activity, you need to know how full of files and directories your hard disk is. If more than about 5Mb is allocated, you should select a branch to back up which contains enough files to fit on three or four floppy disks. A branch or directory extending to some 3-5Mb would be about right for this activity.

First use the command **chkdsk** to see how much disk space is used up.

1   TYPE **chkdsk c:**

```
Volume HD100MB created 06-12-1991 12:24p
Volume Serial Number is 0000-18EF

104114176 bytes total disk space
73728 bytes in 2 hidden files
397312 bytes in 162 directories
90230784 bytes in 4388 user files
13412352 bytes available on disk

2048 bytes in each allocation unit
50837 total allocation units on disk
6549 available allocation units on disk

655360 total bytes memory 576928 bytes free
```

As you can see from the output from **chkdsk**, some 90Mb of my hard disk has been allocated to files. If I were to attempt to make a backup using 3.5 inch HD disks I would need over 60 disks and a spare afternoon. (The **chkdsk** command is covered in more detail in Task 24.)

Change to a directory like **\windows** and list the files in all its subdirectories.

2   TYPE **cd \windows**

3   TYPE **dir /s**

```
Total files listed
     150 file(s) 5268277
```

If I divide the number of bytes of the total files listed, by the capacity of a 3.5 inch HD disk, it comes to just over 3.6. I shall require four such disks to back up the **\windows** branch of my file store.

Activity 18.3 Doing the back up

Now gather all your formatted disks, pens, write-protect tabs and labels.

1   Write a label for the first disk: 'WINDOWS BACKUP DISK #1' and stick it on.

2   TYPE **backup c: a:/s** and put in the first disk when prompted.

3   While the first backup disk is being processed, prepare the label for the next disk:
    'WINDOWS BACKUP DISK #2'

When you see the message: Insert backup diskette 02 in drive A:

4   REMOVE the first disk and, before you do anything else, set the physical write-protection
    by moving the switch or sticking on the metal tab.

5   Put your WINDOWS BACKUP DISK #2 into **drive A** and strike a key to continue.

6   Repeat steps 3 to 5 for BACKUP DISK #3 and so on until the task is complete.

When you have finished you will have a small collection of clearly labelled, write-protected
backup disks. They should be stored away from the computer in a different, secure location so
you won't have lost all your backup disks in the same fire that destroyed the computer!

Backup command switches

There are switches to control the **backup** command (like **xcopy**) so as to make
backups of only those files that have changed since the last backup. This
restricts the number of active files that require backing up.

backup source destination [/switches]

/a   adds files to be backed up to those already on an existing backup disk
          without erasing the existing files. Not the same as **xcopy /a**.

/m   backs up only those files that have changed since the last backup and
          resets the archive flag of the source file like **xcopy /m**.

/d:date   backs up files updated on or after the specified **date**.

/d:time   backs up files updated on or after the specified **time**.

/f:[size] formats the target disk to the default **size** unless specified, e.g. **/f:360**.

/L:[file] logs a backup entry in the default backup log file called **\backup.log**
          unless a different combination of **drive:\path\filename** is specified.

Restoring files from the backup disk

● To restore files that have been backed up using the backup command

Occasionally a disk drive crashes or some other mishap occurs that causes loss or corruption of files on a disk. The damage can be repaired by using the **restore** command to copy files from the backup disk(s) which you put away carefully. Backups which were made using **copy, xcopy** or **diskcopy** would have to be restored using **copy** or **xcopy.**

Normally you use **restore** to copy files from a backup floppy or a series of floppies to the hard disk.

The general form of the command is similar to that of **backup:**

restore sourcedrive: targetdrive: [filename] [/switches]

You must specify the source and destination drives. The appropriate combination of **\path\filename** is used to specify which file(s) or directories from the backup disk are to be restored. You do not have to restore all the files unless absolutely necessary. Before backing up you should delete any unwanted files.

Examples:

```
restore a: c:
```
restores all files from **drive A** to the root directory of **drive C** provided the **/s** subdirectory switch was not used when files were backed up.

```
restore a: c: /s
```
restores all the files from **drive A** to their original directories on **drive C.** If the directories do not exist on **C** they will be created by **restore.**

```
restore a: c:\dos\mouse.sys
```
restores only the file **mouse.sys** to the **\dos** directory of **drive C.**

Restore does not copy the hidden system files **io.sys** and **msdos.sys**

The **restore** command will restore files that were backed up using a previous version of the MS-DOS **backup** command.

Switches

At first sight the switches appear to be almost identical to those of **backup**. Be careful as they can produce different results.

Switch	Restores
/a:date	only files modified on or **after** the specified date
/b:date	only files modified on or **before** the specified date
/e:time	only files modified on or **before** the specified time
/L:time	only files modified on or **after** the specified time
/m	only files updated since the last backup
/n	only files that do not exist on the backup disk
/p	prompts the user for permission to restore files that are read-only or have the archive flag set (i.e. files that have changed since the last backup)
/s	restores subdirectories as well as files
/d	displays a list of files on the backup disk that match the files specified in the **filename** parameter but without actually performing the backup.

Preparing to restore files from your backup disk

First you must delete all the files and directories that you created in Task 17. As you are deleting files on the hard disk, be sure to follow the safe deletion rule you learned in Task 11.

cd \dosguide\docs
dir *.*
del *.*

cd ..\accounts
dir *.*
del *.*

cd ..\memo
dir *.*
del *.*

cd \dosguide
rd \docs
rd \accounts
rd \memo

Activity 19.1 Restoring files from the backup disk

NB Use the backup disk you made in Activity 18.1. Do not attempt to restore from the series of backup disks you made in Activity 18.2.

1   TYPE the command **restore a: c:**

```
WARNING! No files were found to restore
```

Don't panic if you see this rather alarming message. Because you did not include the **/s** subdirectory switch, **restore** cannot deal with the subdirectories that you backed up in the previous Task.

2   TYPE **restore a: c /s**

```
Insert backup diskette 01 in drive A:
Strike a key when ready


*** Files were backed up 15-04-1994 ***
*** Restoring files from drive A: ***

Diskette: 01
\DOSGUIDE\CONFIG.SYS
\DOSGUIDE\HIMEM.SYS
\DOSGUIDE\DOCS\CONFIG.SYS
\DOSGUIDE\DOCS\HIMEM.SYS
\DOSGUIDE\MEMO\AUTOEXEC.BAT
\DOSGUIDE\MEMO\WIN.BAT
```

A cautionary tale about backup and restore

Not long ago a friend came to me in rather a worried state as he had accidentally deleted a very important database file containing over three thousand records. I asked him if regular backups had been made. A set of backup disks had been prepared, one for each day of the week. When he attempted to restore the data file from the Monday backup disk, he followed the instructions and inserted backup diskette 01 in drive A. To his surprise, he saw this error message:

```
WARNING! Diskette is out of sequence
Replace diskette or continue if OK
```

He decided to continue with the restore, and after a short time, disk activity ceased and this message appeared:

```
Restore file sequence error
```

Next he tried restoring from Tuesday's backup disk, and then Wednesday's, but still the same sequence error kept appearing until all the disks had been tried. What had gone wrong?

After finding out from my friend that the database file had been created from scratch, and how every day more records were added to the file, the penny dropped. One backup disk for each day of the week was fine for the first four or five weeks, but one day the database file grew too large to fit on a single floppy disk. By this time he had got used to putting only diskette 01 into **drive A**. When the message **Insert Backup diskette 02** came up he didn't notice the difference. He left diskette 01 in the drive and pressed the **Enter** key, thinking he must have omitted to do so earlier. This caused the last bit of the database file to be recorded over the top of the first part which accounted for the sequence errors. Worst of all, it was not possible to restore any data from the backup disk, which was now thoroughly corrupted.

That is why I recommend that you take each backup disk out of the drive and immediately replace the physical write-protect switch or sticky tab before putting in the next disk of the sequence. You can be interrupted in the middle of the job, or the phone will ring, and it is very easy to get the disks out of order. At least you can't write over an earlier disk in the sequence if you have taken this simple precaution.

MS-DOS 6 Microsoft Backup

The new utility **msbackup** is a complete screen-based package with integral file restore facility.

Before using it you should TYPE: **help msbackup**

The package works with you interactively to help you define the disks, directories and files that require backing up. Your specifications are saved in a file with the **.set** extension. So if you were making a backup of the ACCOUNTS branch of the tree, you would be prompted to save your **msbackup** specifications in a file called **accounts.set**. Then whenever you want to back up that section of your hard disk, all you have to do is type the command: **msbackup accounts**

Protecting against computer viruses

● To minimise the risk of infecting your disks and data with viruses

It would be very remiss to conclude a chapter on disks and security without some mention of that scourge of present-day personal computing, the computer virus. There are no activities included in this task, but I do recommend that you familiarise yourself with the basic facts about computer viruses.

What exactly are computer viruses?

Computer viruses are programs that behave in similar ways to their biological role models. Although of course they cannot infect humans, they can certainly affect humans and I have observed many symptoms ranging from acute anxiety, to rage and finally despair as a result of their depredations.

Viruses live hidden away in an unused part of a disk. Usually this is a place the normal non-technical user cannot access such as the boot sector. When the computer is booted up, the virus is loaded into memory and again it chooses an area where it is well out of harm's way. Once loaded into memory it can monitor various activities that take place and interfere with them according to the degree of maliciousness of its inventor.

How do they spread?

In order to transfer to other computers, the virus copies itself to the boot sector of a floppy disk as soon as it notices one that has been placed into the drive. Viruses can also be carried along with legitimate data that is being transmitted between computers connected together via telephones and modem devices.

The initial spread of viruses is thought to have occurred mainly through early shareware software and electronic mail boxes or so-called bulletin boards where enthusiasts continue to exchange programs, data and messages. Once an infected floppy disk is placed into a drive in your computer there is a very strong likelihood that the virus will transfer to your hard disk. Every floppy disk you then use will probably become infected, and if you exchange disks with friends and colleagues, their computers will become infected in turn.

The analogy with the HIV virus is striking. Computers most at risk are those that have many users, like those in computer rooms in educational establishments. A computer at home with one faithful user who doesn't accept strange disks is not at risk.

What are the effects of a virus infection?

There are as many computer viruses as there are sick programmers with the time to waste. Every year more get added to the list of known viruses, running into thousands. The mildest are just silly, asking you to wish the perpetrator a happy birthday when the program notices that the system date is the same as its inventor's birthday. Even these relatively harmless ones can cause problems, since their very presence can get in the way of a legitimate program and inhibit some critical process with unpredictable results. Other bad viruses can wipe out the contents of RAM memory, erase or corrupt files, attach themselves to files and grow so that the hard disk appears to run out of space.

How can a computer be protected?

There are a number of software utilities available to protect against computer viruses. They can monitor the computer's activities to detect the presence of an intruder and they can also remove a virus from a disk or from memory. The MS-DOS 6 upgrade includes an anti-virus package which scans and removes certain viruses. The package is Central Point Anti-Virus which unfortunately has had a hard time with the computer press. The advice is to continue with other more robust third party packages if you already have them.

If you are responsible for the security of your own data, whether at work or at home, then you should consider the level of risk. If you have to transfer data between machines via floppy disks, or you connect to external bulletin boards or mail boxes, then you should certainly purchase an anti virus package. They are regularly given comparative reviews in the computing press.

The best advice is to avoid exchanging disks with other people. Moreover, unauthorised copying of software is against the law.

If you find your computer is behaving unpredictably, for instance files may disappear, strange messages appear, file listings from **dir** contain unfamiliar characters, then switch off your computer and get the anti-virus software. The longer you leave it, the more havoc will be caused. If you must use the computer, boot it up from the write-protected system boot disk that you made in Activity 14.3. That way there is less chance that the virus will be loaded into memory when the machine starts up.

MS-DOS 6 Anti-Virus software

There is both a DOS version and a Windows version of this program. You cannot use the memory resident DOS version **vsafe** when Windows is running. For both versions there is very good documentation in the MS-DOS 6 **Upgrade Manual**. In addition to this there is comprehensive on-line help available within the package by pressing the F1 key in the DOS version or via the usual Help box in Windows. If you have an anti-virus software package installed, you should check your practice disk for viruses.

Section E
Configuring MS-DOS

Task 21: Investigating the MS-DOS environment
Task 22: Setting the path variable
Task 23: Understanding the system configuration
Task 24: Optimising disk performance
Task 25: Using virtual drives
Task 26: Editing the autoexec.bat file

| Task 21 | Investigating the MS-DOS environment

● To display the current environment
● To set new environment variables

MS-DOS reserves part of the RAM memory for use as a reference area where information can be stored about the way the computer has been set up. This area of memory is called the **environment space**. Both the system itself and also users can set up a number of **variables** that can be accessed when required by programs. Each variable can store a string of characters.

Activity 21.1 Displaying the current environment

The command **set** can be used both to display, as well as to set up or remove, environment variables.

1   TYPE the command **set**

You should expect to see a display looking something like this:

```
COMSPEC=C:\DOS\COMMAND.COM
PATH=C:\;C:\WINDOWS;C:\DOS;C:\UTILS;
PROMPT=$p$g
DIRCMD=/o/p
TEMP=C:\WINDOWS\TEMP
```

Five variables and their contents were listed in the example display. There is an explanation of what it all means on the next page.

Typical environment variables

Exactly which variables you will see displayed by the **set** command and what each of them contains will, of course, depend on the way your particular computer has been configured. Here are some of the more usual environment variables, together with an explanation of their more typical contents.

COMSPEC=C:\COMMAND.COM
The variable COMSPEC specifies the location of **command.com** which is the DOS command processor. In this example, the **command.com** program is specified as being located in the root directory of **drive C**.

PROMPT pg
You have already met the prompt variable in Task 4.3. It stores a string of characters that determine how the command prompt looks. The prompt string **pg** displays the current path, followed by the **>** symbol: C:\DOS>

PATH=C:\;C:\WINDOWS;C:\DOS;C:\UTILS;
In the MS-DOS operating system, external commands or other programs are executed by typing their names. DOS searches the current directory for the command and if the program is there it will be executed. If a path variable has been set up like the one above, DOS will continue to search for the command in each of the specified directories.

DIRCMD=/O/P
This setting tells the **dir** command to display an ordered listing one page at a time. It saves you having to add the **/o/p** parameters each time you type the command. Any suitable combination of **dir** parameters can be similarly preset.

TEMP=C:\WINDOWS\TEMP
The full path of a temporary directory used by **windows** is assigned to the variable called **temp**.

Activity 21.2 Assigning data to new variables

You can make a new variable called **user** which will store your name.

1   Use the command **set user=[name]**, but substitute your own name, like this:

set user=jenny

To check that the new variable has been added to the environment space, use the **set** command without any parameters.

2   TYPE the command **set**

You should see that the new variable **user** has been added to the display.

Activity 21.3 Making a home directory and assigning its path to a variable

Often users have their own personal home directory. In this exercise, first create a home directory in your name, then store its path in a variable that you will call **home**. You should be in the root directory of **drive C**.

1 TYPE the commands **md user**
                                      cd \user
                                      md [name] (substitute your own name in place of [name])

2 TYPE the command **set home=c:\user\[name]**

3 To check your work, TYPE the command **set**

The variable **home** can be used in DOS batch file processing to perform various tasks such as routinely making backups of the files in your home directory. These user variables are usually initialised by the **autoexec.bat** program when the computer is booted up, or by network software when you log in.

Activity 21.4 Cancelling environment variables

To remove a variable from the environment, you set it equal to nothing, like this:

1 TYPE the command **set user=** ENTER

This is called **assigning** a **null string** to a variable.

If you try to write too many variables into the environment, you will see the message:

    Out of environment space

This has to be adjusted by altering your **config.sys** file. Setting up the **config.sys** file is discussed in Task 23, see the SHELL statement.

Troubleshooting

In Activity 21.3, if after typing the command **md** [name] you got the error message:

    Parameter format not correct - [name]

it was because you did not substitute a name of your own choice. Do not include the square brackets which indicate that a substitution must be made.
If you type **set user=[jenny]**, the brackets will be considered part of the string, so watch out!

Setting the path variable

- To investigate the current path
- To set and reset the path

As you saw in Task 21, the path variable contains a string of directories separated by semi-colons. When a command is typed, the DOS command processor attempts to execute it by performing the following tasks:

First it searches the DOS area of memory to see if the command is memory resident and can be executed immediately. If that fails the command processor looks in the current directory to see if the command is stored there in the form of a program file. Remember that program files have the typical extensions:

.com   .exe   .bat

If the search of the current directory fails to find the program, DOS will look to see if the path variable has been set. Suppose the computer has a path variable set like this:

```
C:\;C:\DOS;C:\WP51;
```

In this case DOS will search each of the directories contained in the string. Only if the command is not located in any of these directories will you see:

```
Bad command or filename
```

In the following activities you will investigate the effect of the path variable before learning how to update or reset it. If external commands have failed to work and you have been directed here to Task 22, then Activity 22.3 will show you how to set up a temporary path. If you want to configure the computer to store your new path permanently, then you will have to edit **the autoexec.bat** file. This is covered in Task 25.

Activity 22.1 Checking the current path

1   To display the current setting of the path variable, TYPE the command **path**

The output from the command should look something like this:

```
C:\;C:\DOS;C:\NORTON;C:\WIN;
```

If your computer has not been set up with a path variable, the result after TYPING the command **path** will be the message:

```
No path
```

Activity 22.2 Cancelling the path variable

To cancel the path variable you make the path equal nothing, or the **null string**.

1 TYPE **set path=** (ENTER)

2 TYPE **path**

   no path

Make sure you have your practice disk in **drive A**, then make **drive A** the current drive:

3 TYPE **a:**

4 TYPE **tree**

   Bad command or filename

DOS can no longer find the **tree** command because you have cancelled the path.

Activity 22.3 Setting a new path

First find where the **tree** command is located.

1 Change back to the root directory of **drive C** by TYPING:

   c:
   cd

2 TYPE **dir tree*/s**

Suppose that the **tree** command is in a directory called \DOS. You must set a path that will scan the root directory and then the DOS directory.

3 TYPE **set path=c:\ ;c:\dos**

If your **tree** command is in some other directory you should substitute that directory's name instead of \DOS

Notice that each element of the path variable is separated from the next by a semi-colon.

Activity 22.4 Restoring the original path

When you switch on the computer, the path is usually set by a program called **autoexec.bat**. However, you can run the **autoexec** program at any time by typing the first part of its filename. The program is normally located in the root directory of **drive C**.

1   First change to the root directory of **drive C** by TYPING:

    c:
    cd

2   TYPE **autoexec**

3   TYPE **path**

    You should see a path string like this, e.g. C:\;C:\UTILS;C:\WIN;C:\PCTOOLS;

What to do if there is no path at all

In Task 4 you should have used the **tree** command to look at the directory structure of your hard disk. If the command did not work it was probably because your computer does not have a path set up, so DOS does not know where to find the command. You should work through the activities in Task 22 so that you understand how the path variable works. Activity 22.3 will show you how to locate the **tree** command and then set a path so that DOS can find it.

Note that this is a temporary procedure because when you switch off the computer the contents of memory variables are lost. In order to set up the path automatically every time the computer is switched on, a path statement must be included in the **autoexec.bat** program file.

If there is no path statement at all in the **autoexec.bat** program you will have to add a line to the program file. The other possibility is that there is already a path statement, but it does not include the directory where the **tree** command (and presumably certain other DOS external commands) is located. In this case you will need to update the path statement in the **autoexec.bat** program.

Adding lines and editing **autoexec.bat** is covered in Task 25. **Do not** attempt to use a word processor to edit a program file unless you fully understand how to create an unformatted ASCII file.

The path statement enables DOS to locate program files. The programs themselves may have their own problems locating data files. To get round this, other directories can be added, or **appended**, to the working directory by the **append** command. For instance, word processor document files located in the directory **\text\book** can be accessed as if they were in the **\word** directory by typing the command **append c:\text\book**. This is another statement that can be made more permanent by including it in the **autoexec.bat** program.

Understanding the system configuration

- To investigate the current setup of the **config.sys** file
- To practise configuring the system
- To use the new MS-DOS 6 diagnostics utility

Every user likes to have his or her computer set up in a way which reflects a personal working style, or optimised to suit their particular programs. In spite of working at a so-called **personal** computer, in practice most users put up with configurations inherited from previous users, or from dealers or suppliers if the computer is new. A good dealer should consult with you about the way you want the machine set up and will probably install other software for you as well. In the workplace, where computers are shared, whether it's the office or a computer lab in a school or college, compromises have to be struck between the demands of different users. As PCs have become more and more powerful so the options for configuring the computer have grown in number and complexity. This Training Guide aims to give a basic introduction for the benefit of the non-technical user.

Hardware and software configuration

The hardware configuration refers to the physical resources of the computer such as the amount and type of memory, the processor type, what disk drives there are, their type and capacity. This information has to be stored so that programs know what resources are available and how to address them. The hardware configuration mostly lives in a reserved part of memory called CMOS RAM which is powered by batteries so that it is not lost when the computer is switched off. The CMOS RAM is updated by a special utility program called **setup** which is beyond the scope of this Training Guide.

Software configuration is the next stage at which the functions of your PC can be more finely tuned to the requirements of yourself and the software you want to run. You have already looked at some of the settings of your computer in previous tasks. You will have discovered which version of DOS has been installed; whether the date and time have been accurately and permanently set; whether the file store has been sensibly structured into a coherent directory system; whether the root directory contains the working minimum of files or whether it is overflowing with files that probably ought to be somewhere else!

Most of these aspects of a system can be controlled by commands you have already met. Other features control the way the keyboard behaves. Do you get a pound sign when you press (SHIFT-3) or do you get the 'hash' # sign? Are the " and @ keys reversed? Is the date in European or American format?

When the computer is booted up it reads the hardware configuration in CMOS memory, followed by statements in the **config.sys** file. Further adjustments are made when the **autoexec** program runs.

Activity 23.1 Looking at the config.sys file

You learned how to locate and display the contents of a file in Task 8. If you have forgotten how to do this you should follow the steps below:

1 First locate the file by TYPING **dir config.sys /s**

Config.sys is often installed in the root directory, or the subdirectories \SYS or \DOS.

2 Change to its directory by TYPING **cd** or whatever is appropriate.

3 Use the **type** command to display the contents of the file.

   type config.sys

You should see something like this:

```
BUFFERS=32
FILES=30
DEVICE=ANSI.SYS
DEVICE=MOUSE.SYS
SHELL=C:\COMMAND.COM /P /E:256
LASTDRIVE=Z
COUNTRY=44,,\SYS\COUNTRY.SYS
```

Explanation of config.sys statements

BUFFERS= x   e.g. BUFFERS=32

This statement tells DOS how much Random Access Memory to reserve for **disk buffers** that store data on its way between the working memory and disk drives. Each buffer is a 512 byte unit of memory and can store the contents of one disk sector. Buffers hold parts of files that have already been accessed and are likely to be required again, thus saving another disk operation. The processing of complex directory structures and applications that require a great deal of disk activity is speeded up by having adequate buffer space.

FILES= n   e.g. FILES=30

Many applications need to have simultaneous access to a number of files. Windows programs are particularly greedy in this respect and typically require some 30 files open at any particular moment.

Although specifying a large number of buffers and files does improve system performance, this is achieved at the expense of memory. Since memory is now a less valuable commodity, it is likely that most computers of the 1990s will have enough RAM for you to be generous in your allocation.

DEVICE=[drive:][path][driver]

e.g. `DEVICE=ANSI.SYS DEVICE=C:\SYS\MOUSE.SYS`

The config file can have a number of **device** statements each of which loads a specified driver. Peripherals such as keyboards, video displays, mouse pointers and so on need interface programs called **device drivers** that tell the computer system how the particular device should work. Typical device drivers include:

ANSI.SYS which controls the screen and the way simple graphics and colour are handled by the older style character-based software such as accounting packages.

PRINTER.SYS which enables certain foreign language character sets to be printed on a printer that supports them.

HIMEM.SYS which is a memory device driver that stops programs from being loaded into the same area of extended memory.

RAMDRIVE.SYS which enables RAM memory to be used as a **virtual** disk drive. Such disks are also known as **ramdisks** or **silicon** disks. They operate much faster than a real magnetic disk and judicious use of them can speed up applications that access disks intensively. The trade off is that they tie up a substantial chunk of RAM, so you must careful that sufficient RAM remains for the application software.

Warning! Data held on virtual disks is not permanent and is lost when the computer is switched off. Data should therefore be copied to a real disk at regular intervals.

A well organised directory structure may well have device drivers and other system files collected together in their own subdirectory called \SYS. Certain .sys files will be supplied with MS-DOS, but manufacturers of peripherals such as mice, scanners and network cards will supply their own proprietary drivers.

SHELL=[drive:][\path\filename][/parameters]

The **shell** statement is normally used to specify the home directory of **command. com.** The environment switch /E:n can be used to release **n** number of bytes of extra memory for the use of environment variables. The /P switch tells DOS to keep **command.com** permanently in memory so that it is not displaced by rogue software. Here is an example of a shell statement:

`SHELL=C:\COMMAND.COM /P /E:512`

The command processor is also known as the **shell**, because the relationship between the operating system and the outside world of the user can be visualised as a shell that separates the boundary between the kernel of a nut and its environment. The basic, or **default** MS-DOS command processor is enabled by the program **command.com** which loads and processes all the familiar memory resident commands like **dir** and **cd**.

However, other operating systems such as Xenix, Pick, DRDOS and OS/2 have their own command processors that can be invoked by substituting the appropriate path and filename into the shell statement.

LASTDRIVE=[letter] e.g. `LASTDRIVE=Z`

If you need to access many disk drives, use virtual or memory drives, or access other drives across a network, you will soon run out of letters to call them by. The default drive letter is E. The statement **lastdrive=Z** enables any letter to be used as a drive name.

COUNTRY=n

Each country has a code number; the country code for the UK is 44. The combination of country code and the **country.sys** driver looks after the keyboard and makes sure that you get the pound sign and no surprise letters with strange äccents. If your **.sys** files have all been collected together in one subdirectory, the country statement will have to specify the location of **country.sys**, e.g.

`COUNTRY=44,,\SYS\COUNTRY.SYS`

Activity 23.2 Making your own config file

It is advisable to experiment first before attempting to install your own **config.sys** file on a hard disk. For this exercise you will need the floppy boot disk you made in Activity 14.3.

Remove any physical write-protection and place your boot disk into **drive A.**

1 TYPE **a:**

To construct a simple **config.sys** file you can use the DOS text editor, or the **copy con** command you met in Task 10.

2 TYPE **copy con config.sys**

    buffers=30
    files=32
    country=44,,\sys\country.sys
    device=\sys\ansi.sys
    device=\sys\ramdrive.sys 64 128 64
    ⌞Ctrl-z⌟ ⌞ENTER⌟

Activity 23.3 Booting from your amended boot disk

Now you can try out the effect of your new config file.

1   REBOOT the computer with the boot disk in drive A. You can either do a **warm boot** by holding down (Ctrl) (Alt) and pressing the (Delete) key, or press the **reset** button.

You will see error messages saying that the various device drivers are bad or missing. This is because your new config.sys file has told DOS to look for them in a non-existent directory called \SYS.

2   TYPE **md sys**
       cd sys

3   COPY all the **.sys** files from your hard disk. Locate them using **dir *.sys /s** and then use the **copy** command, e.g. **copy c:*.sys**

4   REBOOT the computer again.

If all goes well you should see the display telling you that the **ramdisk** has been installed correctly as **drive D** (or **E** if you already have a **drive D**). You must not expect to see the normal working environment that you are used to because a number of other features are set up by the **autoexec** program which is absent from your boot disk.

Troubleshooting

If there is a problem it will probably be caused by the RAMDISK driver. You may not have located and copied the driver to the **\sys** directory of your boot disk; it may not be installed on your machine at all, or you may have a different version called VDISK, in which case go back and substitute the word **vdisk.sys** in place of **ramdrive.sys** in the preceding activities.

Reset your computer

Before moving on to the next Activity or Task, take the boot disk out of **drive A** and **reboot** so as to restore your computer to its normal settings with the config file that is installed on your hard disk.

Activity 23.4 Using the system diagnostics program

Another screen-based utility has been released with MS-DOS 6 called **Microsoft System Diagnostics**. It provides technical reports and specifications on every aspect of the computer.

1   Change to the root directory of **drive C**

2   If you have a colour monitor, TYPE **msd**

3   If you have a monochrome monitor you should TYPE **msd /b**

You will find yourself in a full screen display with labelled buttons corresponding to the various parts of the computer about which you need technical data. Try selecting various buttons. You will be able to access all the configuration details easily and you can browse through them at your own pace.

Activity 23.5 Printing an msd report

It is possible to generate either a summary or a complete report which can be printed immediately. Alternatively, the output can be saved to a file for later reference.

1   To send a summary report to the printer, TYPE:

   msd /s prn

2   To send the summary to a file, substitute a filename of your choice in place of **prn**, e.g.

   msd /s ibm12.msd

You could call your file after the make of your computer and give it the extension **.msd** to remind you that the file is an **msd** report.

For a full report, use the **/p** switch in place of the **/s** switch. As the report is about 11 pages long, my advice is to look at it on screen first.

3   TYPE **msd /p con**

You can see the full list of switches and their functions by typing **help msd**

It is advisable to print the full report at some convenient time when you are not busy. If the computer breaks down, this piece of documentation could be very useful to the service engineer.

| Task 24 |

Optimising disk performance

● To scan a disk and check it for errors
● To recover lost data
● To defragment a disk

The external command **chkdsk** displays a report on the status of a given disk of any type, as well as displaying error messages relating to corrupted files. If the /f switch is used, **chkdsk** will attempt to salvage files.

Activity 24.1 Checking out your practice disk

1   Place the disk in **drive A** and TYPE the command:

chkdsk a:

If the disk is in good order you should expect to see something like this:

```
Volume Serial Number is 2B0E-0EFF

362496     bytes
total disk space 71680 bytes in 2 hidden files

   1024     bytes in 1 directories
 214016     bytes in 9 user files
  75776     bytes available on disk

   1024     bytes in each allocation unit
    354     total allocation units on disk
     74     available allocation units on disk

 655360     total bytes memory
 512912     bytes free
```

The essential information here is that the total disk capacity is 362,496 bytes, i.e. 360K. Roughly 71K is allocated to hidden system files, 214K is used up in 9 files, and about 75K space is left on the disk, which is not a lot. The last two lines of the report tell you how much conventional memory has been used up. Even if your machine has 8 Mb of extended memory, this will not be acknowledged by **chkdsk**.

Activity 24.2 Checking the hard disk for errors

1   To report on the status of the hard disk, log on to **drive C** and TYPE **chkdsk c:**

There is always a possibility that there may be some **bad sectors** on the hard disk. If this is the case you will see an error message like this:

```
6144 bytes in bad sectors
```

Ignore this message, frightening as it may seem. Bad sectors are a physical problem and the operating system will avoid such areas and data will not be written to them.

If the computer is accidentally switched off when files are open and work is up on the screen, it is possible that files can be corrupted and end up in 'limbo'. In this case **chkdsk** reports the error like this:

```
Errors found, F parameter not specified
Corrections will not be written to disk.

16 lost allocation units found in 4 chains.
Convert lost chains to files, (Y/N)? N  ◄────(Press N for no at this point)

32768 bytes disk space
        would be freed
```

Activity 24.3 Recovering lost files

If you find that there are some lost chains that can be converted back to files, you can use **chkdsk** with the **/f** switch, e.g. **chkdsk a:/f**

When you are asked the question: `convert lost chains to files(Y/N)?`

Pressing **Y** for yes will cause the file to be recovered. You will see the line:

```
32768 bytes in 1 recovered files
```

added to the usual **chdsk** display. If you type **N** for **no**, that area of the disk is returned to the File Allocation (FAT) Table as free disk space.

Warning!

When files are recovered by **chkdsk** they do not reappear with their original names. Recovered files are given temporary filenames of the type FILExxxx.CHK where xxxx is a number in the range 0000 to 9999, e.g. FILE0001.CHK. The file must then be renamed to its original name. Use the **type** command to see if the file consists of text. If it consists mainly of unreadable characters you should discard it, as it was probably a binary code program and will now be corrupted.

Optimising disk performance

When files are first written to a new disk, they occupy adjacent, or **contiguous** disk blocks. As a new computer gets older and the hard disk fills up with more software and the user's own data files, the speed of the disk drive becomes noticeably slower. Loading and saving files seems to take ages and the disk drive 'chatters' to itself while the red light flashes for rather too long. This is caused by **disk fragmentation**. As old files are deleted to make way for new ones, they leave spaces all over the surface of the disk. When a new file is written, it is allocated to the first available free space, but this may not be large enough to accommodate it. The rest of the file will then be tucked into various other free areas of the disk until it has all been allocated.

In directories where there has been a lot of activity, large files will often be scattered over many **non-contiguous** areas of the disk. Performance will then slow down or **degrade** because the disk drive heads have to be repositioned all over the surface in order to read the file from its fragmented blocks.

Activity 24.4 Checking for disk fragmentation

If you run **chkdsk** followed by a parameter containing filenames or the wildcard *, a list will be displayed of any files that are spread across two or more **non-contiguous** disk blocks.

1   Try this on your practice disk by TYPING the command **chkdsk a:*.***

and you will probably get the message:

```
All specified files are contiguous
```

This is because there are relatively few small files and there has been no need for any of the files be split up into non-contiguous blocks.

If you use a database program, you could try running **chkdsk** on files in that directory, e.g.

```
C:\>chkdsk \db4\*.dbf

C:\DB4\CUSTOMER.DBF
     Contains 2 non-contiguous blocks

C:\DB4\STOCK.DBF
     Contains 8 non-contiguous blocks
```

I have come across users who have been near to despair at the snail-like pace of their database applications. By using **chkdsk** I have found individual files spread over as many as 32 non-contiguous blocks. If a database index file is heavily fragmented, the response time for a query increases to a quite unacceptable level.

Defragmenting the file store

There are various ways of reorganising the disk so that all the files are relocated to contiguous blocks. As a simple, relatively 'quick fix' you can use a combination of DOS commands as described below or you can use a **disk compaction** program. If you have MS-DOS 6, there is now a disk compaction utility **defrag**. Alternatively, you can use one of the longer established standard packages such as PCTOOLS and NORTON UTILITIES. If you have MS-DOS 5 installed you will have to use one of these disk utilities, or the method described below.

Warning!

Before defragmenting your disk using any method, **back it up** (at least your most important files) to floppy disks or to a tape streamer.

Activity 24.5 Simple file store reorganisation

This is an easy method of fixing a badly fragmented subdirectory.

1   Use **backup** or **xcopy** to copy the files from the fragmented directory to floppy disks.

2   Create a new directory which will be on a new part of the hard disk.

3   Restore the files from the backup disks to this new directory.

4   Test the new directory using **chkdsk**, and by running the programs there.

5   If you are happy, then you can delete the fragmented directory.

Troubleshooting

If you have problems it could be because there are programs which have been set up to refer to the old directory. Or, the disk is so full that there is no room for both the fragmented directory and the new one. In this case, you will have to delete the fragmented directory before restoring files from your backup.

If you have a tape streamer and you are confident in its ability to make reliable backups, then you can reformat the hard disk and restore the files from the tape.

MS-DOS 6 defrag program

Defrag is a full-screen disk defragmention utility from Symantec's **Norton Utilities**. It is a fully-documented product with on-screen help facilities. Before running it you should type **help defrag**

Using virtual drives

● To substitute a drive letter for a path

The term virtual is often used in computing to mean a device that is not real. Thus a virtual disk has no physical existence, but the operating system can be configured to regard blocks of RAM memory as if they were a disk (see Activity 23.2 where a **ramdisk** was set up).

Another trick is to substitute a spare drive letter for a long directory path.

Activity 25.1 Substituting a letter for a directory path

Set up a new directory path on your practice disk in **drive A**.

1 TYPE **a:**
       cd

2 TYPE **md text**
       cd text
       md book
       cd book
       md part1

You should now have a subdirectory that could be used to store all the text files that would make up part one of a book. The path is **a:\text\book\part1**

3 Now substitute the spare drive letter **D** for the subdirectory path by TYPING:

   subst d: a:\text\book\part1

You can test your virtual **drive D** by redirecting the output of **echo** to a file called **chapt1**.

4 TYPE **echo practice file > d:\chapt.1**

5 Log on to your new **drive D** and list its contents by TYPING:

   d:
   dir

The output from **dir** should look something like this:

```
Volume in drive D is HD100MB
Volume serial number is 1B05-172D
Directory of D:\

chapt.1    14   21-09-94 3.12p
```

Notice that the disk volume label and serial number are the same as those of **drive C**. Your new **drive D** is, after all, really a subdirectory of **drive C**.

Activity 25.2 Resetting a substituted drive

You can use the command without any parameters to report the presence of any substitute virtual drives.

1 TYPE **subst**

```
D:=> A:\TEXT\BOOK\PART1
```

2 To remove a substituted drive, use the **/d** delete drive switch, e.g.

d: /d

If you were logged on to your virtual **drive D** when you included the **/d** switch you would have seen the error message:

```
invalid parameter -d:
```

You cannot remove a substituted drive when you are logged on to that drive any more than you can remove the current directory.

Troubleshooting

1 Choice of a suitable drive letter

You must use a letter that is not already in use by any existing physical or virtual drives. Unless your machine has been configured otherwise, the only drive letters available are A to E. In practice this leaves you with only the letters D and E. You can alter this default setting by including the statement:

```
lastdrive=z
```

in the **config.sys** file. This enables any letter of the alphabet to designate a drive, whether real or virtual.

2 Restrictions on virtual drives

You cannot use **subst** on a networked drive. Neither can the commands **backup, restore, format, label, chkdsk** and **recover** be used on your virtual drive. For instance if you were to use the **label** command you would see the error message:

```
Cannot label a SUBSTED drive
```

Command syntax

subst [drive1:][drive2:][\path][/d]

e.g. `subst m: c:\user\joe\database\files`

● To investigate and edit the autoexec.bat file

The autoexec.bat file

By now you should be more familiar with the configuration of your computer and you will have looked at some of the statements that make up a typical **config.sys** file. Another important part of the startup mechanism is the **autoexec.bat** program. Individual DOS commands that alter the working environment are collected together into this **batch program** and executed automatically immediately after the **config.sys** file is loaded.

Batch programs can be used to automate processes that would otherwise have to be executed by typing each command individually. You may have come across a similar idea in applications software such as Word, WordPerfect, Lotus 1-2-3 and Excel, where certain tasks are automated using collections of commands and keystrokes called **macros**.

The Microsoft Editor

A simple screen-based text editor is supplied with MS-DOS 5 and 6. (It is essentially the same as the editor supplied with the two Microsoft programming languages, Quick C and Quickbasic.) So far you have been using **copy con** to create simple files. However, if you need to change or edit a file, it is better to load the file into the Editor and make use of the various editing functions. It is not the purpose of this Training Guide to explore the MS-DOS Editor in any detail, but it will get you started and show you how to load, change and save a file. If you need more information there is extensive coverage in the **Microsoft MS-DOS User's Guide and Reference**.

You will need to have at least basic word processing skills to use the Editor.

Activity 26.1 Loading the Editor

1   Remove any physical protection from your floppy boot disk and put it into **drive A**.

If the Editor is located in C:\DOS and the path has been set up as in Task 22, you should be able to start the Editor by typing the command **edit** followed by the full filename of the file you want to make:

2   TYPE **edit a:\autoexec.bat**

You will find yourself in an empty text window, like the one illustrated on the next page. It is rather like being in a word processor.

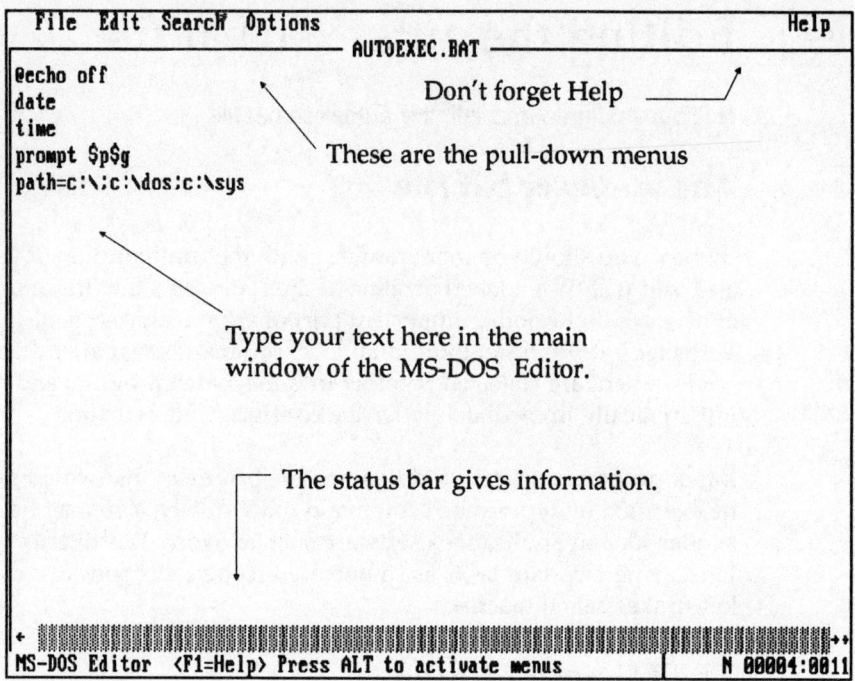

```
   File  Edit  Search  Options                                    Help
                        ──── AUTOEXEC.BAT ────
 @echo off                              Don't forget Help ───────/
 date
 time                           These are the pull-down menus
 prompt $p$g
 path=c:\;c:\dos;c:\sys




                               Type your text here in the main
                               window of the MS-DOS  Editor.



                             ┌─ The status bar gives information.




 ← ▓▓▓▓▓▓▓▓▓▓▓▓▓▓▓▓▓▓▓▓▓▓▓▓▓▓▓▓▓▓▓▓▓▓▓▓▓▓▓▓▓▓▓▓▓▓▓▓▓▓▓▓▓▓▓▓▓▓▓ ←→
 MS-DOS Editor  <F1=Help> Press ALT to activate menus        N 00004:0011
```

Activity 26.2 Entering and editing text

The cursor should be at the top left of the empty window.

1 TYPE the following lines:

```
@echo off
date
time
prompt $p$g
path=c:\;c:\dos;c:\sys;
pause
cls
```

If you make a mistake, you can use the cursor keys to move about from line to line and from character to character. You can use the (Insert) and (Delete) keys to make changes just as you do in any other word processor.

Activity 26.3 Saving your work

When you have finished Activity 26.2, EXIT and SAVE the file.

1 HOLD down the (Alt) key and PRESS **F** for file, or use the mouse to point at the **File** option at the top of the screen.

2 SELECT the Exit option using the cursor keys or mouse.

The Save dialog box will pop up as shown in the example screen below.

3 Press the (Enter) key to execute the default option which is <Yes> to confirm that you do wish to exit and save the file.

The status bar at the bottom of the screen tells you how to move between options using the (Tab) key. There is also fairly extensive help available at each critical point as well as more general help when you press the (F1) key.

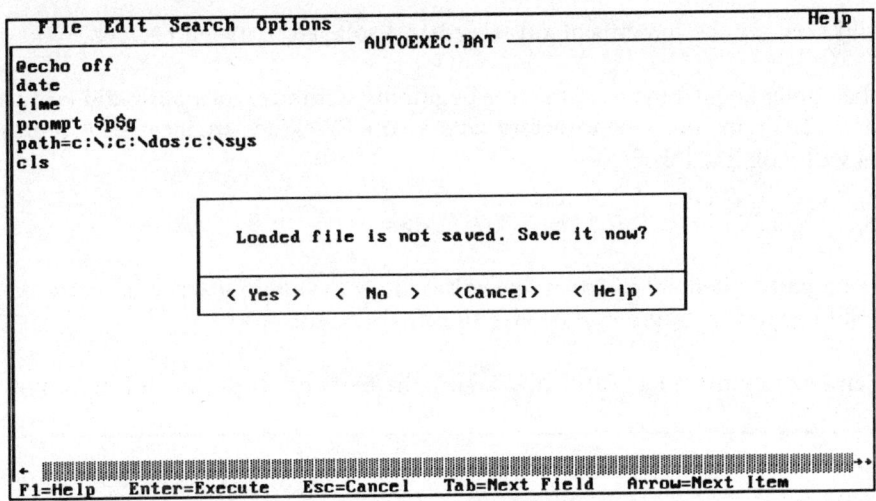

Activity 26.4 Testing your autoexec.bat file

1 With your floppy boot disk in **drive A**, PRESS the **reset** button, or HOLD down the (Ctrl) (Alt) (Delete) keys.

You will now be able to see what happens as your **autoexec.bat** program runs.

The first line of the program, **@echo off** prevents each command of the batch program being echoed to the screen. The **date** and **time** commands enable the user to check that the settings are correct and to update them if necessary. The path statement is vital to ensure that commonly used DOS external commands or other utilities can be executed outside their home directories. The **pause** command enables the user to read any system or error messages before the screen is cleared by the **cls** command.

Activity 26.5 Changing the path statement

Do not experiment with the **autoexec.bat** file itself. Copy the file to your floppy boot disk and try out the following activities in safety. If all goes to plan you can copy the edited file back to the hard disk when you've tested your program.

1 Remove any physical write-protection from the boot disk and place it in **drive A**.

2 Log on to **drive A** and copy the **autoexec.bat** file from the root directory of **C:**

   a:
   copy c:\autoexec.bat

3 TYPE **edit autoexec.bat**

If the command does not work, you should log back on to **drive C** and type the command **dir \edit.com /s**. When you have located the whereabouts of **edit.com**, change to its directory and TYPE **edit a:\autoexec.bat**.

You should now see the contents of **autoexec.bat** displayed in the edit screen.

4 Use the cursor keys to move to the line beginning with the word **path** and edit the path statement so that it includes the directory where your DOS files are located. A typical path statement will look like this:

```
path c:\;c:\dos;c:\utils;c:\windows
```

If there is no **path** statement in the autoexec.bat file, you should insert one. It can be one of the earliest lines in the program, after **@echo off**.

5 Save and exit by pressing (Alt) **F** and taking the Exit option as you did in Activity 26.3.

Activity 26.6 Checking and installing your edited autoexec.bat program

1   With your floppy boot disk in **drive A**, PRESS the **reset** button, or HOLD down the
    [Ctrl] [Alt] [Delete] combination of keys.

2   TYPE the command **set**

Check that your modified path has now been made permanent by changing to **drive A** and
typing an external command like **chkdsk** or **tree**.

3   TYPE the commands:

    a:
    chkdsk

If you're happy that the path is now correctly set, and that you have not disturbed any other
statements in the autoexec files, you can proceed to install your amended version.
First make a backup of the original **autoexec.bat** and then remove the **read-only** flag that
should have been set to protect it. Finally, copy the new version of the file from **drive A.**

4   TYPE the commands:

    c:
    cd
    copy autoexec.bat autoexec.old

    attrib -r autoexec.bat
    copy a:\autoexec.bat

5   Remove the floppy boot disk from **drive A** and replace the physical write-protection.

6   Reboot the computer as before and then repeat steps 2 and 3 to make sure that you have
    edited the path correctly. If you are satisfied that everything is in order, finish off the
    whole procedure by resetting the attrib flag to read only:

    attrib +r autoexec.bat

Troubleshooting

If the computer does not start up in the usual way it could be because you have
inadvertently messed up the **autoexec.bat** file. In this case you should re-install
the old autoexec file and try the whole thing again. Re-install the original file
like this:

    c:
    attrib -r autoexec.bat
    copy autoexec.old autoexec.bat
    attrib +r autoexec.bat

Glossary of computing terms

ASCII American Standard Code for Information Interchange. An international code for 128 characters, letters, numbers and punctuation marks as found on the standard computer keyboard. A further 128 graphics characters are also defined.

Backup An additional copy of a file or disk stored on another disk or tape for security purposes.

Batch program or **file** A list of MS-DOS commands that are executed without the user's intervention.

BIOS Basic Input Output System. The lowest level of system software stored in Read Only Memory.

Bit The abbreviation of binary digit, 0 or 1, which is the smallest unit of information in a digital computer.

Bold, boldface Heavier version of a typeface.

Boot Abbreviation of **bootstrap**, from the expression 'hauling oneself up by the bootstraps'. The procedure for starting up the computer.

Byte A binary data 'word' made of eight bits. A byte can store one character or machine instruction.

Character Letters, numbers, punctuation marks.

Cold Boot Restarting the computer by switching the power off, then on again.

CPU Central Processing Unit. The part of the computer that processes instructions, performs arithmetic and logic, and controls the memory and resources of the system.

Cursor A marker on the screen that indicates the position of a character.

Default Preset functions and parameters.

Destination disk A disk to which files or directories are to be copied.

Directory A section of a disk with a user-defined name in which a group of related files are stored.

Disk head The part of the disk drive mechanism that floats over the disk surface and which reads and writes data to and from the disk.

EOF The abbreviation for the End of File marker.

ESC A key that enables the user to exit from the current activity in a software program or package.

Filespec The specification of a group of files using the wildcard characters, e.g. the **filespec sales??.*** would specify both **sales10.dat** and **sales05.doc**
A **filespec** can include a drive and directory path.

Font A set of characters in a particular style of typeface, e.g. Palermo, Times New Roman.

Fragmentation When files on a disk are dispersed over a number of different locations.

Gb, Gbytes, Gigabytes A unit of memory consisting of approximately one billion bytes.

Hardware The physical parts of the computer system including the CPU and peripheral devices.

I/O devices see Peripheral devices.

Internal commands MS-DOS commands that are loaded into memory when the computer boots up. They remain memory resident unless displaced by applications software.

K, Kilobytes A unit of memory consisting of 1024 bytes.

Log on In MS-DOS to change to a different drive or directory.

Lower case The set of 26 characters a,b,c,...,z

Mb, Mbytes, Megabytes A unit of memory consisting of approximately one million bytes.

Monitor The computer screen or Visual Display Unit (VDU).

Off-line When a peripheral device or disk is not connected or loaded.

On-line Peripheral devices like printers and disk drives are said to be **on-line** when they are connected directly to the CPU.

Parameter Data or further instructions that follow a command word.

Path The full specification of a subdirectory, starting from the root directory of the drive, e.g. C:\USER\JOE\DOCS

Peripheral devices Input/Output devices such as disk drives, printers, mouse and keyboard.

Program A set of stepwise instructions telling the computer how to process a given task or tasks.

Prompt A signal from the computer telling the user to respond by typing in data or a command.

RAM The abbreviation for Random Access Memory, used to store programs and data while they are being processed. The contents of RAM are lost when the power is switched off.

Read-only A file is Read-only when it cannot be changed or deleted.

Redirect symbols Enable data to be transferred between a DOS command and a file, e.g. more<read.me

ROM Read Only Memory Memory that cannot be changed or erased.

Scrolling When the screen display rolls on so that more information can be seen.

Source disk A disk from which files or directories are to be copied or moved.

String A sequence of characters such as those that make up a **path**. See **path**.

Subdirectory A directory below another directory in the tree structure.

Switch An optional character placed at the end of a command line that fine tunes the command. e.g. **/p**

System files Program files used by the operating system to control the computer.

Tape streamer A magnetic storage device for backing up large disk drives.

Target disk (or drive) A disk to which files or directories are to be copied.

Typeface A collection of characters in a similar style. See **font**.

Upper case The set of 26 characters A,B,C,...,Z

VDU Visual Display Unit The screen that displays output from the computer.

Virus A program that infects disks and memory and can cause corruption of data and programs.

Wildcard The characters * and ? that are used to substitute for groups of characters in filenames that are to be processed by a DOS command.

Write-protect Physical protection to prevent a whole disk from being changed or erased.

Index

MS-DOS command words are shown in bold.

OPEN LEARNING SERIES

This user-friendly series provides clear, step-by-step instructions to all aspects of each package. Many college courses are now based upon **open learning** techniques and an increasing number of people are developing word processing skills at home or in the office.

- purpose written open learning material
- task centred, with helpful guidance notes
- clear, easy-to-follow instructions
- each unit is self contained to allow 'dip-in' learning for those requiring spot revision
- a problem-solving section in each unit answers questions for those learning alone

Titles include:

WordPerfect 5.1 for DOS and Windows
Microsoft Word for Windows 2.0
Lotus 1-2-3 for Windows
dBASE IV 1.5

Ask for the titles in the *Open Learning Series* in your local bookshop. Alternatively, contact our Marketing Department:

Pitman Publishing
128 Long Acre
London WC2E 9AN
Tel: (071) 379 7383

FROM START TO FINISH

This major new series offers its readers complete and thorough mastery of the most widely used databases, spreadsheets, desktop publishing and word processing packages.

Suitable for use by absolute beginners, each title will take the student through every aspect until they have achieved a significant level of competence. The format and structure of the books enable students to follow one learning strategy (and use only one book) for preparation for the series of examinations they need to pass.

- covers all functions and applications of each package
- geared to the needs of the student who wishes to pass examinations after each learning stage
- a one-book solution to learning a package from elementary to advanced levels
- accompanying 3.5" and 5.25" disks are available for each title

Titles include:

dBASE IV 1.1
Lotus 1-2-3 for Windows
Word 2.0 for Windows
PageMaker 5 for Windows
Quark Xpress 3.1 for Windows
WordPerfect 5.1 for Windows